SHORT MONOLOGUES FOR ACTING CLASSES

Lexington Avenue Press

Copyright © 2020 Frank Catalano

All rights reserved.

ISBN (Print): 978-1-54398-172-8
ISBN (ebook): 978-1-54398-173-5

SHORT MONOLOGUES FOR ACTING CLASSES

Frank Catalano

TABLE OF CONTENTS

INTRODUCTION	1
WHAT IS A MONOLOGUE?	4
WHAT KINDS OF ACTING CLASSES ARE THERE?	6
WHY DO I HAVE TO DO A MONOLOGUE IN MY ACTING CLASS?	7
HOW DO I SELECT A MONOLOGUE FOR AN ACTING CLASS THAT IS RIGHT FOR ME?	9
TREAT YOUR MONOLOGUE AS IF IT WERE A SCENE	11
WHAT'S THE BEST WAY TO MEMORIZE MY LINES AND CREATE A PHYSICAL LIFE FOR MY CHARACTER?	13
PERFORMING A MONOLOGUE FOR AN ACTING CLASS - HOW TO CREATE AN IMPLEMENTATION STRATEGY.	14
CREATING A PERFORMANCE DYNAMIC - HOW TO MAKE A CREATIVE BOX TO PLAY IN	15
HOW TO PLAY EACH MOMENT AS IF IT WERE A PIECE OF A LARGER MOSAIC	16
USING "WHAT IF?"	17
HOW TO CREATE THE "MOMENT BEFORE"	19
HOW TO CREATE "NOW" USING SPECIFIC OBJECTIVES AND BEATS	19
HOW TO CREATE THE "MOMENT AFTER"	22
HOW TO BEGIN A MONOLOGUE AT AN ACTING CLASS	24
WHO SHOULD I LOOK AT WHEN I PERFORM A MONOLOGUE IN AN ACTING CLASS?	26
HOW DO I END MY MONOLOGUE IN ACTING CLASS?	26
HOW TO HAVE FUN AT ACTING CLASS	28

THE MONOLOGUES

#1 SIGMUND FREUD AND REPRESSION	33
#2 SOMEONE	34
#3 ANIMAL REPULSION	35
#4 WEARING GLASSES	36
#5 LUCKY	37
#6 THE TAT	38
#7 IRON CITY – 1957 COUNTRY SQUIRE	39
#8 KONG ISLAND – 1931	40
#9 BABYSITTING	41
#10 SNAPSHOTS	42
#11 INVISIBLE	43
#12 TEST DAY	44
#13 THE FULL COLLEGE EXPERIENCE	45
#14 THE CLASSICS	46
#15 BRIDGES	47
#16 THE MESSAGE	48
#17 THE 13TH FLOOR	49
#18 SOLITARY	50
#19 PARTY ANIMAL	51
#20 STRIPES	52
# 21 ELEANOR RIGBY	53
#22 MY LOCH NESS	54
#23 SHE PUT HER KNEE UP	55
#24 A LINE IN THE SAND	56
#25 INDIFFERENCE	57

#26 JUST THE FACTS	58
#27 ASCENDING	59
#28 STEPPING OUT	60
#29 WITTY DIALOGUE	61
#30 DAY TO DAY MATTERS	62
#31 HELLO	63
#32 SIXTIES ROCK AND ROLL DREAM	64
#33 YOU NEVER LISTEN TO ONE WORD I SAY	65
#34 FATAL ATTRACTION	66
#35 PASTORAL	67
#36 DECAY	68
#37 JULIET'S UNDELIVERED NOTE TO ROMEO	69
#38 DRUNKEN SUPERMAN	70
#39 THE SOLILOQUY	71
#40 PEE SOUP	72
#41 FIVE SMALL BITES	73
#42 WOLF	74
#43 ROPE	75
#44 THE BACKSIDE OF YOUR HEAD	76
#45 DOG'S FEET SMELL JUST LIKE POPCORN	77
#46 WHITE SILHOUETTE	78
#47 DONUTS	79
#48 TO DIE FOR…	80
#49 COFFEE PEOPLE	81
#50 A. X.	82
#51 GOODBYE	83
#52 CONFESSIONS OF A SERVER	84
#53 THE BARBERSHOP	85

#54 LAUNDRY	86
#55 HOLD DOWN THE SEATS	87
#56 SITTING SOMEWHERE OUTSIDE	88
#57 YOUR SPIRIT	89
#58 - THANK YOU	90
#59 MAN'S WORK	91
#60 WOMAN'S WORK	92
#61 DILLY DALLY	93
#62 STEPPING ON THE CRACKS	94
#63 PEACE	95
#64 THE VIETNAM WAR AND THE FORT HAMILTON LAMENT	96
#65 PALACE HOTEL- NEW YORK CITY	97
#66 HOW DEEP TO DIG A HOLE	98
#67 LISTENING	99
#68 BAD HAIR DAY	100
#69 DOG PEOPLE AND CAT PEOPLE	101
#70 - LIVING INSIDE A HEFTY BAG	102
#71 VISUAL AUDITORY	103
#72 WASH YOUR HANDS	104
#73 LITTLE WHITE LIES	105
#74 BLOCKED	106
#75 - HAPPY FOR YOU	107
#76 CONTEMPLATION OF SELF	108
#77 DREAMING OF PARIS	109
#78 ROMANTIC	110
#79 DUMB WAYS TO DIE	111
#80 IF I COULD ONLY BE THIN	112

Introduction

As an author, I have written several monologue books including **ART OF THE MONOLGUE**, **HOW TO SELECT AND PERFORM MONOLOGUES and SHORT MONOLOGUES FOR AUDITIONS** - all three have focused on the performance of a monologue as a creative presentation with a specific environment and situation. This current volume focuses on the presentation of monologues specifically for acting classes. The difference here is that the actual selection and presentation of the material is focused more upon the development an actor's abilities in an audition rather than a performance an acting class. **Why short monologues?** As an acting teacher, I have always advised my students *"less is more."* What does that actually mean? In this case, I want the student actor to focus specifically on a given purpose in the presentation of the monologue as it relates to the development of acting skills. The given purpose of a monologue for an acting class is to provide the teacher a sample of your acting abilities, your demeanor, ability to take direction and ultimately to determine what you will focus on in the class. It is very different from using a monologue for an audition. A casting director is rarely if ever going to have you perform a monologue if they are reading people for a specific role. They will just have you perform the actual lines of the character that you are reading for. A director of a theatre company, a university theatre school, an agent or manager might want to see how you perform prepared material. They would want to see how you create the moment on your own so they can have an idea of the kind of actor you really are and how you would fit into their company or agency. But let's get back to the acting class. When you select a monologue, select something that's brief, to the point and gives your acting teacher an idea of who you are and what you can do. An actor should have at least two short contemporary monologues (one comedy and one dramatic) ready to go at all times. A contemporary monologue is one that derives from the 1950's to present day. Most of the of the monologues contained in this book are contemporary. If your acting class covers the classics, you want to be totally prepared and can add at least one or two short classical monologues to your acting arsenal. **Classical" monologues** are speeches taken from plays that can derive from ancient Greece, Shakespeare to the early twentieth century depending upon how they are defined by your acting teacher.

If you select a contemporary monologue from a popular movie or play found on the internet, you will present yourself at a slight disadvantage. The danger in presenting familiar material will invite comparison. Most acting teachers will have seen and heard other student actors do these same monologues. As you perform, your teacher and the class will be thinking about the last student that presented the same material. How did they do it? How does your interpretation differ? Which one is better? You don't want them thinking about another student performance. You should select monologues that are new and fresh to their ear. Show them something new that is a perfect fit for just you. Something, that they can only imagine you performing. It should show what you can do emotionally, intellectually and physically and most importantly be brief and to the point. Brief and to the point means about one to two minutes. Remember, your performance is a sample of what you can do, not the whole performance.

Presenting a monologue in front of a whole class is also like an audition, you want to bring into the group a short sample of your acting ability or to showcase a specific aspect of your talent. If your strong suit is emotional roles, prepare a short emotional monologue. If it's physicality, then prepare something that relies centrally upon your ability to move within the space. This is no secret. Acting teachers and students prefer shorter monologues for class presentations. Why? This allows both the teacher and the student the ability to focus on specific acting issues rather than restating them over and over again within a cumbersome presentation. Usually, your acting teacher (just like a casting director) pretty much knows what they need to work on with you after the first minute of your presentation. So, why not dazzle them with a presentation that's short and sweet. Give just enough to make them interested but leave them wanting for more. If you can do that, you are where you need to be.

This book contains eighty individual monologues that can be performed by both male and female characters. There is an equal mix of comedy and drama and all are within the one to two-minute time range. You might be thinking, which one is right for me? Find a monologue that you can closely connect to either on an emotional or intellectual level. Put yourself in the space as the character and let the monologue do the rest of the work. Ultimately, the right monologue for you is one that showcases your unique talents and that can be only attributed to you. It becomes your monologue in the eyes of your teacher and class. Think of an acting class monologue as a means to end that is going to exhibit what you can do and where you would fit into the composition of the class. As a class exercise it's going to give your acting teacher a specific insight about who you are, your talents and what areas of acting you need to work on.

Lastly, monologues like everything else, are subject to your tastes and needs at any given moment. Don't be afraid to try many different monologues as your creative growth progresses or you feel you need to do something different. Make this book your source for the magic that you will do. Go back to it again and again whenever you feel there is a need for it.

What is a monologue?

The American Heritage Dictionary defines a monologue as a long speech made by one person, often monopolizing a conversation. You may be thinking, I already know that, tell me something I don't know. Okay, a monologue when spoken can reveal a small part of a character's soul. Think of those thoughts in which you have spoken aloud to someone or yourself. The words you speak come from within you and have special meaning. Unless, you count as monologues leaving phone messages, placing your order at the automated machine at Jack in the Box or trying to talk on the phone to customer service at your bank. It is true that a monologue is a speech made by one person but really it is a lot more than just that. What the person says in his/her speech should be worthy of speech itself to be considered a monologue. What am I saying? It should be a speech connected in some core way to your character's intellectual, emotional, spiritual and physical state. If it is not that, then it is not a monologue. It is whatever it is: leaving a phone message, ordering a cheeseburger or trying to find out why your check has bounced.

Within the framework of a performing arts presentation, a monologue is one person speaking for an extended period alone or with other characters upon the stage or within a camera shot. The speech can be the character's thoughts spoken aloud to himself or herself, to another character, to the audience or an object or entity. How a monologue is presented has a lot to do with the reality of the universe the character lives in and to a greater extent the point of view or creative framework of the presentation. I am defining point of view as **how** a creative work is presented to its audience. Several years ago, I attended a production of William Shakespeare's Hamlet at small theatre in Los Angeles. I sat in the first row about three feet from the actor who played Hamlet as he uttered those famous lines **"To be or not to be..."** I had experienced this soliloquy dozens of times before within a representational framework where the Hamlet character reveals his inner thoughts by speaking to himself out loud. In this particular production, the actor who played Hamlet turned toward me and asked the famous question, **"To be or not to be?"** At first, I wanted to blurt out like Robert Di Niro in **Taxi Driver, "Are you talking to me?"** But, somehow thought it might not be appropriate. So I said nothing. But I did give him a look of acknowledgment. As if to say, **"I heard that… and that is definitely a question to consider."** For the rest of the show, the audience kept looking at me as if they wanted me to do or say something. I never did. I am not saying that it was wrong to present the Hamlet soliloquy in this manner. The creative framework of that particular production of Hamlet was *"presentational"* meaning it had the characters (including Hamlet) acknowledging the presence of the audience. At that particular performance, I unwittingly assumed that role. I could have chosen to respond verbally to Hamlet, but I chose just to acknowledge his look. However, we can say that Hamlet acknowledging the audience in the middle of his soliloquy was done on purpose and was part of the creative framework of the presentation. The creative framework, which defines a presentation of a play or film to an audience, usually falls within the point of view of the Director.

The Director of a play or film sets the framework and tone of how the material will be presented. When you choose to perform a particular monologue, just like a director, you must choose **how** you will convey the reality of your character and situation to an audience. You must ask yourself, what do I want to achieve within my creative framework and what is the desired outcome? I am not suggesting that you perform your acting class monologue directly to your teacher or classmates. I think it is best to create a framework that keeps them separate from the reality of your character. This allows the teacher make notes on your performance, sit back and see what you can do and it enables your classmates to observe you without being part of the presentation. You don't want them; feeling forced to react to your gaze or directed line toward them. It will make them uncomfortable and lessen your chance to showcase what you can do. Your creative framework in presenting your monologue should be focused on how to best present the reality of the character you have created within a given universe and to connect that character to your individual talents. The purpose of an acting class monologue is not to solely show your acting ability, it should also illustrate how you create a character, interpret lines and present them to an audience.

Now that we have discussed what a monologue is and how it should be presented, let's get back to our original question. Why do we have to do monologues in an acting class anyway?

What kinds of acting classes are there?

There are a variety of acting classes you may consider taking. If you take an Introduction class as part of a college program, you will be introduced to the basic skills required to be an actor which would include: Introduction to theories and development of acting skills through drill in fundamental stage techniques, character building, and in class performance of memorized prepared monologues, scenes and analysis of dramatic literature with emphasis upon developing performance skills. Other classes may focus on character development, physicality, working on camera, improvisation, commercials, cold readings, voice acting or career preparation. Other classes, mostly private ones, do a little bit of all of these things on an ongoing basis. Some invite casting directors or agents as part of their curriculum. The important thing to remember is that you must always have a clear-cut idea of what the goals of the class are and make sure they fit within your own personal targets. Failure to do this will result in you wasting your time. Also, check out the teacher philosophy and class composition before you sign up. If the class has a lot of undisciplined noncommitted students or a poor teacher, this is not the class for you. Sometimes the teacher might be knowledgeable but their teaching philosophy is not a good fit for you. There was one acting teacher who had the practice of berating students every time they presented a performance in class. He would tell the students they were worthless, had no talent and would never be successful unless they studied with him. This is an acting class you don't want to take. The best way to see if an acting class is the right fit for you is to "audit" the class.

This usually means you would be allowed to sit in the class (not participate) and observe. If the teacher doesn't allow audits, then find another teacher. If it's a college class, drop it and enroll in another acting class.

Why do I have to do a monologue in my acting class?

A fellow colleague at one of the colleges where I teach once told me that he assigns monologues early in the semester to "weed out" the people who are not serious about being in the class. Why is that? He went on by saying if you assign a monologue early on, it forces the student to memorize a large chunk of dialogue and present it to the class. I will agree that one of the most daunting tasks for beginning students is learning lines and memorizing and performing a long monologue scares some of the not so serious students away. I don't agree with that reason for assigning a monologue. However, I do feel it is valuable to assign a short, to the point monologue for students early on in the class because it enables students to learn how to trust their choices. I want them to present a concise idea in a minute or less and not worry about whether they memorize every word exactly. I also want students to approach a monologue as a scene rather than a speech that has to be rattled off as quickly as possible. Performing a monologue is more about the actor performing it than an audition for a particular role in a play or movie. Most casting directors, when reading actors for a particular project, like to have the work performed from a specific script either as a cold reading or a memorized screen test. So having one or more monologues prepared is **not** going to land you a specific role in a film or television program. In order to do that, you are going to have to do a **cold reading** of the material from the project. If you cannot use a monologue for a film or television audition, why bother working on one?

The answer to the question of why we do monologues is to be able to show your acting teacher and down the line a casting person, agent or performing arts school representative your ability to perform prepared (rather than cold) material and offer such content within a clear-cut presentational format. In this book, I have developed primarily shorter pieces to be used for acting classes. In a classroom / studio setting, an actor can work on specific challenges of character creation, line memorization, nervousness and physicality. As an acting class exercise, the student wants to present a monologue that is a concise sample of his/her work which highlights their ability to memorize dialogue, create the intellectual, emotional, physical and spiritual state of a character. It should also exhibit their creative ability to present prepared material from a specific point of view. The **"how" and "why"** we do monologues then is clear. This is a sample of how you can interpret material when you have had a time to prepare it and present it within a specific creative framework. However, just because it is prepared, you are not expected to create a whole play or movie. What is expected is for you to provide a short sample (one to two minutes) of your creativity and talent to a specific audience. Who is this audience? It can your acting teacher and fellow students and later be an agent, producer, and an artistic director of a theatre ensemble, an admissions committee at an acting school/college or a director. However, the **who** is not as important as the **how** you create it. The first step in this process is the selection of the right material.

How do I select a monologue for an acting class that is right for me?

By Casting Type

No matter how versatile you think you may be as a performer, an acting teacher and later casting directors or agents will only see you playing roles that they feel fall within your appropriate casting type. Casting type is a combination of factors which can include your: age, physical stature, hair color, ethnicity, speech patterns or accent and generally the way you appear to most people most of the time. You should select a monologue that is **type appropriate** for you. That is, if you are female age twenties, you should not select a character that is an older woman. Pick a character that is generally your own age. Acting teachers who are familiar with how theatre and film are cast will help you identify your type. Once you establish this, agents and casting directors will look to identify you as a particular type. Remember, your type doesn't stay the same forever. As you grow older, your physicality or demeanor changes, so will your type. Some actors intentionally want to change their type so they may evolve into different kinds of roles.

By talent and skills

Your monologue for an acting teacher is a way of showing them where you are creatively. It is best to select a class monologue that shows your strongest skills rather than do something for the first time that may be a stretch for you. If you have never done Shakespeare, your first monologue in class should be something that you can do. If you are asked to try Shakespeare for an assignment, that is a different story. The best rule is always lead off with your strongest presentation. If you are preparing a monologue for an audition for entrance into a school or theatre ensemble, you want to select material that will highlight what you do the best. If you have difficulty in showing intense emotion, then stay away from those types of monologues until you can perfect the skill to perform them. Select monologues that will highlight what you do best. Note that some acting schools require selection of monologues from existing plays either from a specific list or within a date range. For example, they may request preparation of two monologues: one classical such as Shakespeare, Moliere, or Sophocles and one contemporary within the last fifty years. Always start with the monologue that you do best. If you feel your strongest talent is comedy, then lead with that. If you feel your strongest talent is drama, then lead with that.

Compatibility with career or artistic goals

Select monologues that are compatible with the goals you are attempting to achieve. If you are taking an acting class to address nervousness in front of an audience, then pick one that addresses that issue. Approach your acting class as if you were studying math or science. Formulate in your mind what you specifically want to learn how to do and then focus on it. Articulate this goal to your acting teacher and then ask them to help you achieve it. If you are auditioning for a commercial agent, a crisp, short, high-energy (but not too happy) monologue would probably be best. A longer dramatic narrative or verse monologue would not be the best choice for a commercial agent but might work in perfectly for an audition for a theatrical agent (film and television), theater company or college performing arts program.

Purpose or Skill Goal

An acting teacher may ask you to select a monologue, so that you can work on a specific acting goal such as anger, physicality or listening. For example, if you are asked to work on a specific emotion, select a monologue that will stretch your abilities in that area. When you present your monologue in acting class, remember it is not a speech.

Treat your monologue as if it were a scene

Many actors hate performing monologues because they feel it is just a speech and not a true representation of their acting ability. They believe that performing a monologue does not provide the opportunity to show an acting teacher their ability to react to another character. We have stated earlier that a monologue is a longer speech where a character can speak to himself or herself, another character or object or the audience. When you create your monologue know **who** you are speaking to and don't forget to create their presence for the audience. When you say a line give the other character, audience or yourself if it is soliloquy an opportunity to hear and respond to it. When Hamlet utters ***"To be or not to be..."*** he's asking himself that question and should think about how he would answer it.

Your monologue dialogue should not be just a wall-to-wall recitation of lines but instead a well thought out pattern of dialogue, which takes into consideration the intellectual, emotional, physical and spiritual universe of the character.

Let's stop here a moment and define these four-character attributes.

Intellectual:

This is what your character intellectually believes within his/her universe. It goes to the core of the things they do. It could be as simple as Democrat or Republican but it can go deeper about their understanding of the universe, they live in. Characters are often thrust into situations that force them to make decisions based upon logic rather than emotion. This is often the case in business decisions where statistics or numbers are involved. However, an intellectual choice can also be based upon a belief system within the character. Some factor causes them to calculate and then act upon a decision that is centered around facts and data rather than feelings.

Emotional:

This is what your character feels about themselves and the other characters they relate to in their universe. What emotion dominates their existence and how does it affect what they do and what happens to them. Certain situations demand an emotional response. What you feel becomes more important than what your character thinks or intellectually rationalizes in a given situation. In 1916, there was a shark attack on a little boy in an inland Florida lagoon. It was unbelievable to think that a shark could swim that far inland from the ocean. But it happened. As the shark attacked the seven-year old, an adult man jumped into the water and attempted to pull him to safety. The shark killed them both, but there is more to it than that. The underlying motivation for the rescuer was to save the boy despite the danger of being torn apart himself. Perhaps it was fear itself that drew the man into the water. This was the incident that inspired the JAWS movie and was based upon an emotional response.

Physical:

How does your character physically interact with the universe they live in? How do they move? How do they interact physically with other characters? Much of our physical response to the world is filtered through our culture and the times we live in. You could be on a subway car in New York City just inches away from another individual. Actually so close to them that you could smell what they ate for breakfast but not think anything of it because the physicality of that space and situation makes it so. You could take the same physical situation and place it on a line at the supermarket in Los Angeles and you would perceive anyone that close to you as invading your space. A character's physical interaction with the universe that surrounds them can also be influenced by culture or time period. What is acceptable in one culture or time period may not be acceptable in another.

Spiritual:

What are your character's values which go beyond religious conviction to the core of their belief system? Your character's moral core and how they perceive what is right and wrong within their universe. Certain characters find themselves on a journey of discovery and their motivation is centered on that journey. Certainly, Don Quixote's quest in Man of La Mancha would be an example. But your character doesn't have to be on a life-long quest to find the meaning of life to have a spiritual motivation. The spirituality can simply be an exploration of aspect of your character's inner being.

Certainly, try to allow whomever your character is speaking to react to what is being conveyed just as you would in a two-person scene. Your character speaks the lines in the monologue and then allows the other character or the audience to respond. Even if they are not making a sound, you need to give them time to react. If you do this, your presentation will be more than a mere recitation of the words of the script in which you race through the lines before you forget them. Allow whomever you are speaking absorb what you are saying and doing. In addition, don't forget to create them in the space. Look at them, react to them and allow them to react to what your character is doing within the piece.

What's the best way to memorize my lines and create a physical life for my character?

I have heard many actors complain: **"I knew the lines when I was driving my car but now, that I'm on the stage, I just can't remember anything."** When I hear this type of statement, I know what they have forgotten to do is create a physical life for their character. They recite their lines over and over again like a speech while they are driving on the freeway. What they are doing is training their brain to memorize these lines while they drive and fall into the trap of thinking about a monologue as just a speech rather than a slice of a character's life. This means that the moment that we experience your character speaking, it is part of a much larger mosaic. When preparing to perform a monologue don't forget to create the physical life of the character. What I mean is the physical connection to where your character is and what they are doing as they speak. Creating a physical life will go a long way in helping you to memorize the lines. Your ability to memorize what your character is saying will be connected to a specific physical reality and idea. Your brain will connect what is being said to a specific movement and place. However, you cannot move without purpose. What kind of universe does your character live in and how do they move within it? A character's universe has everything to do with the actual space from which they speak, the time period they live in and the **who** they are speaking with. If your monologue is a soliloquy, which takes place in a graveyard, and your character is speaking aloud to themselves, this is different from a speech talking to your best friend over a cup of coffee.

Performing a monologue for an acting class - How to create an implementation strategy.

WHAT IS AN IMPLEMENTATION

I want you to start thinking like a producer and develop an implementation strategy as a plan to create a framework or foundation to build your monologue. The implementation strategy becomes the concept for presentation. Whatever the purpose of your monologue your preparation for presentation should include an implementation strategy. You may think it is the director's job to create the framework of the character's physicality and emotion and that you should not have to concern yourself with the details of how it will be presented. The truth is that the **who and the how** are indelibly connected. It is like the chef who labors over the preparation and ingredients making up a particular dish, forgetting presentation and just throwing his creation onto a paper plate. In that very act, the chef negates the creative process that taken place before. An actor is no different; consideration of presentation is just as important as character preparation. While an actor cannot control all aspects of presentation, the development of an implementation strategy will create a foundation for the actor to rely upon. In an acting class, you have total control of what you produce viewing in your class. Show your acting teacher that there is some thought about what you present and what you want to share with an audience.

Creating a performance dynamic - How to make a creative box to play in

The dynamic of any presentation takes into consideration all of the physical characteristics of the performance space, the performer's relationship to that space, the distance of the intended audience to the performer, the composition of the intended audience, the surrounding reality of the performance and ultimately the purpose of the performance itself. The dynamics of any given performance can change as the physical characteristics of the space change. While it is virtually impossible for any performer to know totally the dynamic of every performance in advance, it is possible to develop a strategy of presentation, based upon what elements are available.

For an acting class, you should be somewhat familiar with the presentation space, the distance of presentation to the audience, the acoustics, lighting and physical location of the audience. I teach acting at several different types of studio spaces and stages. One space I teach in is in the shape of and "L" with class members sitting in front and to the left of the performance space. Once of the challenges of presenting in this type of configuration is that the student actor must make a special effort to visually include both audience spaces. The monologue cannot just be directed toward the spot where the teacher is sitting. Instead the student actor must open up the presentation so that both sides of the performing space are included. Another space I have a class in, is a larger 500 seat proscenium theatre space. In this example, the actor must project into that space so that all of the class members in the rear portion of the seating can hear what is being said. In addition, the physicality of the performance must be open enough for the last row to know what is going on. If the monologue is intimate in nature, the student must still project enough for everyone to be included. For an audition you can only assume the dynamics of the space and distance to the intended audience. You might be asked to present your monologue in an office setting, a conference room, or an empty stage. The best strategy is to develop a plan for all three and be prepared for any variation you might encounter. In an audition dynamic, the person you are presenting to may be looking for a specific element and not your total performance. They also may be multi-tasking (making notations, conferring with an associate or looking at your resume) while you are in the midst of your performance. Lastly, the reality you attempt to create might be interrupted by an outside source such as a telephone, people entering the space or the casting person themselves.

How to play each moment as if it were a piece of a larger mosaic

The **Presentation Dynamic** you create is literally the creative box you get to play in. It is the creative framework, which is made up of your character's world, and the actual physical elements within your specific performance environment all rolled into one. It could be an acting class studio, a stage, a camera angle, a casting office, or on set location that your character must evolve within. Once you have established this creative framework, there is a multitude of possibilities that are present within that dynamic at that particular moment in time. The important element is that the student actor make specific choices rather than play all things. If your choices are wrong, your acting teacher will work with you to make better decisions about how to present your monologue. The important thing is that you bring something for them to experience. Allow them to react to your choices rather than bringing nothing to the presentation. A student actor once told me that they were a blank page waiting to be directed. That may be one choice. But I think a better choice is to bring something and let your acting teacher respond to it.

Using "What If?"

You have made the choices detailing **who, what, where and when**. Now, let your character ask him/herself the question: "**What If**" one of these choices weren't so? Example: **You are Romeo quietly watching Juliet standing on her balcony.**

Who: A Montague (who falls in and out love) and enemy of the Capulet's

What: Spying upon Juliet (a Capulet) as she speaks her private thoughts

Where: The Capulet's orchard, Verona - a place he should not be.

When: Nighttime after the Capulet feast.

Romeo sees the love of his life but cannot muster the will to speak. As she speaks each line, he falls deeper and deeper into silence.

He succumbs to his fear and gets up to run away when at the last possible moment, despite his fear, he hears Juliet say:

Romeo, doff thy name,
And for that name which is no part of thee
Take all myself!

When Romeo hears this, his fear, vanishes in an instant, and he speaks! Why? He knows he can get it all.

I take thee at thy word:
Call me but love, and I'll be new baptized;
Henceforth I never will be Romeo

Using the "**What if**," you are choosing to play the moment as if this time, in a play that we all know, it will be different. You are playing this scene and speech as if Romeo was going to walk away and somehow this play, at this moment in time would be different than any other Romeo and Juliet that has happened before. The key to playing the "**what if**" is that your character must believe it and more importantly the audience must believe that the **"what if"** is going to change the outcome. Fight the logical inclination to say to yourself, **this is Shakespeare or this is the text, it cannot be changed**. I am not suggesting a change in text, only a change in intention. We often play the end of the scene because there is a preconceived notion by both performers and audiences as to how it all turns out. We need to recreate that notion in the form of "**what if.**" Let the audience sit on the edge of their seats and wonder if that maybe just this time, at this moment, Romeo just might walk away. What would happen then? Using this approach makes your work unpredictable and interesting.

How to create the "moment before"

Where have you come from and what has just happened the moment before?

Within the reality of your character, what moment has the character just left before they entered the moment of your monologue? What was significant about that moment and how has the moment before influenced the intellectual, emotional, physical and spiritual state of your character during the monologue? Within this creative framework, the actor then can convey the thoughts of the character, as they would appear in the full presentation of the work. Playing the moment before the lights go up or the camera rolls then allows the audience to catch your character in the midst of their existence living their life in its entirety.

How to create "now" using specific objectives and beats

What is your character's main objective?

By speaking the words of the monologue and living the moment, what does your character desire to have happen when they finish speaking? Ask yourself, **why** is my character saying and doing this? What is your character's desired outcome? How will you manifest this outcome?

What are your character's sub objectives? Mark them as individual beats.

Are there smaller objectives or beats your character must overcome in order to achieve their main objective? A beat could be a small section of the dialogue or movement within the monologue.

Create a series of beats within your monologue to identify your sub objectives. For example, what would Romeo's sub objectives be?

Beat #1   Romeo sees the love of his life but cannot muster the will to speak.

Beat #2   As she speaks, he succumbs to his fear and gets up to run away.

Beat #3   At the last possible moment, despite his fear, he hears Juliet say:

> **Romeo, doff thy name,**
>
> **And for that name which is no part of thee**
>
> **Take all myself!**

Beat #5   He stops. When Romeo hears this, his fear, vanishes in an instant.

Beat #6   He speaks.

> **I take thee at thy word:**
>
> **Call me but love, and I'll be new baptized;**
>
> **Henceforth I never will be Romeo**

What are the obstacles in the way of achieving your objectives?

In the course of events leading up to, during and after the completion of the monologue, can you identify any obstacles, which are preventing your character from achieving his/her desired goals? Are these obstacles generated externally (literally physical elements) or internal (obstacles created from within your character) which prevent them from their objective? Identify these obstacles and create ways to acknowledge and overcome them.

What is going on at this moment?

At the very moment the monologue begins, what is actually happening? If you took a snapshot of this moment, what would be its title? If you enter your home holding a bouquet of flowers, kiss your wife and hand them to her, and then after giving them to her, you tell her that you have lost your job, what is the title you would place under this moment? It can be called many things, perhaps "**losing my job**" or **"loss"** but it would not be called "**Handing her the bouquet**" because that action is not what is really going on. It is just an action, which is part of the overall moment. So ask yourself, what is really going on in your character's universe at the moment your monologue begins.

When is this moment in time?

Once you have established what the true moment is, then address the question is "**when**" is it? Using the example described above, the moment can be described as morning, day or night but more helpful would be the moment after I lost my job or late at night after I have been walking for hours, because I didn't know how I would tell you. It is literally a definition of **"now."** Once you understand this, you will know what to play. But also understand that **"now"** is constantly changing as the moment evolves. Now is almost indefinable because it is constantly changing. It is truly a moment to moment situation.

Where are you? What is the space for your character?

Even though you may perform your monologue in any number of nondescript spaces, make a decision for your character about specifically where this moment is taking place. Is it at home, on the bus, in an elevator, on a podium in front of a thousand spectators? What is the space? Is it small and confined, larger than life or somewhere in between? Do not confuse this with the Dynamic of Performance (that is more concerned with the physical properties of the actual performance space) the **"where are you"** question addresses solely the reality of the character's universe rather than the performance space. Make specific decisions about the space your character occupies when they begin to move and speak.

How to create the "moment after"

Where are you going after now?

If your character is in a particular space in a particular moment, where will they go next? Is it somewhere specific? Create a concept of motion. Let your words in the monologue and the physical life you have in the moments you create propel you to the next.

Everybody likes to know where they have been and where they are going

I am not asking you to predict the future. However, your character and the audience, in a larger sense, should have some idea about where your character is going intellectually, emotionally physically and spiritually as a result of the monologue being spoken. Everybody loves to peer into the future and know, if even briefly, what the next moment will bring. Even if you don't really have a clear-cut idea of all of it, give your character and your audience a taste of what may come next. An audience, will say, **"Okay, I have watched and listened to you, now what's going to happen next?"** Answer the question: **"Now that I have spoken these words, this is what's going to happen next."** You have to show them how it's going to be and take them along with you on your journey.

"What has happened during this journey?" After all that has been said, has your character changed? If your character has spoken aloud to himself or herself another character or the audience, has this auditory and physical expression of their inner thoughts changed them in anyway? It may be a minute change, but it is a change, nonetheless. What happens next? You as the performer and your character have to answer the question: How has the universe changed and what will happen next? From an audience perspective, we all want to know what's going to happen next. You do not have to write new lines to your monologue but there has to be a sense that something will follow.

How do you play this?

We have come full circle. Your character must have some resolve intellectually, emotionally, physically and spiritually that connects to what is going on within their universe and where it will go in the future. These are choices you need to think about and make before your presentation.

How do you show this?

The way your character contemplates on what they have just spoken in the monologue, or how they react emotionally, or how they physically accommodate the change. Your monologue does not end when the character utters the last line. It ends when the **audience experiences the character's reaction to the last line.** The audience wants a sense of the significance of what has transpired and glimpse of what will be as a result. That is what keeps them invested in your character, they want to know and be part of the progression of what is going to happen next.

When Macbeth speaks the last few lines of his soliloquy, the audience has had a glimpse of his tormented soul and has seen the shadow of the murder that is to come.

Macbeth

I have no spur to prick the sides of my intent,
but only vaulting ambition,
which o'erleaps itself and falls on the other

When Macbeth utters the last line **"And falls on the other,"** the very moment after, we can see the murder that is to take place within his eyes. He exits with a resolve that is clear to us all when he walks off the stage. The audience knows, he has changed and because of this resolution, something significant is going to happen next. He is going to kill the king and we have witnessed the creation of this decision.

How to begin a monologue at an acting class

You have done your preparation, what about the monologue itself? When you enter the classroom or studio space, get a sense of the room. What is the energy level of the people inside? Where are they sitting? In front of you, on the side or both? How large is the space? What is the distance between where you will perform and the people watching you? What is the acoustic quality of the space? Where is the light and are there any seats or other set materials in the space? Adjust to any deficiencies on the fly. If it is a stage and there is an object that will be in your way from a previous presentation, it is okay to use it or move it out of the way. Try to make the space as accommodating for your performance as you can. Make the space your own as you create the universe of your character.

If you are required to speak before, you perform your monologue or do a verbal set up which might include the monologue title and a little bit of background about the source material and setting, try to be as concise as possible. Try not to use words like **"um" or "like."** Instead, be very specific and state the name of the source material and a short summary of the portion of the source material that you are performing and what (if anything) is unique about it. You can prepare this in advance and memorize as part of the overall presentation. If the situation calls for you to go right into your monologue take your time to create the universe that your character lives in. Once it is time to start the actual performance portion of your monologue assignment, make sure you allow some time to separate the reality of the **"assignment presentation and set up"** and the reality of the "**universe of the character**" you are to perform. Don't be a **good soldier** and go directly from a talking to your class into a character. You will not totally achieve the transition and your performance will seem uneven and full of distractions. Before you speak, take a moment to let your character's universe surround you. Don't do warm ups, stretch out or lower your head toward the floor as you **get into character** then suddenly face forward as the character in a totally different physicality. This caveat may seem elementary but I have seen acting students do it all the time.

Remember that your monologue does not begin with your first line. It begins with the moment **before** the first line, which causes your character to react and say those words. A monologue can even begin with a physical action or creation of an emotional or physical state by the character. If you are playing Hamlet, ask yourself what causes this character to speak the line "**To be or not to be…**" Hamlet just doesn't speak those words because Shakespeare wrote them. There is an underlying moment that occurs before the lines are spoken that drives the character to speak those words. When your character speaks those first words of your monologue, let them be a reaction to a previous intellectual, emotional or physical moment. This can be a previous moment in the play, film, or something the audience has not even seen. How you play this reaction to a previous moment has all to do with your character's intellectual, emotional, physical and spiritual connection. Ask yourself the question, what does my character **"think"** about this situation, how does my character **"feel"** right now and how does my character respond **"physically"** to this place and situation at hand. And what are your character's beliefs about the nature of their universe and what is right and what is wrong? Once you have answers to these questions, you will have something to play.

Who should I look at when I perform a monologue in an acting class?

Your character can speak to themselves aloud, to another character or to the audience. However, most individuals involved within the casting selection process do not like to be included in the reality of the presentation. They want to be free to make notes and just experience what you are doing. Some acting teachers direct their students to speak at an imaginary space **over the heads**. I don't like this practice because it is distracting to watch and does not allow the teacher or class to connect to your character. Better, if you are directing your monologue as a soliloquy, direct your comments and actions to yourself. If you are speaking to another character, create a space for that character that your teacher and classmates can easily see. This can be an empty space on the stage or a chair or set piece. If you are addressing the class as a whole, create a similar empty space or spaces within the audience area. In this way, the teacher can choose to participate when they want to but also be free to look down and make notes about you or your performance. Ultimately, I am not one for rules, if you perform your monologue directly to your acting teacher, you will not fall through a hole in the floor. You can do anything you want to do to create the best reality for your specific monologue.

How do I end my monologue in acting class?

In a typical production setting, when your monologue is completed the lights might fade or another character might speak. In a film, another character can speak; they could cut to the next scene or fade to black. In an acting class setting, you will not have any control over the space in which you will perform. There may be harsh lighting; exterior noise or it may not be a performance space at all. I have seen several methods of ending a monologue that I suggest that **you not do.** The first, at the end of the monologue, the actor just bows their head toward the floor as if to say, **"it's over - you can applaud now."** As you can imagine this unnatural ending is abrupt and solicits an artificial applause and response from the class and teacher. Applause belongs in a theatre performance, not an acting class. The second method, at the end of the monologue the actor says the word **"scene."** This is a verbal cue spoken to the teacher indicating that the monologue is over. This method is unnatural and creates an abrupt almost jarring quality. In addition, actors who use this method of ending have a tendency to physically comment upon their work when they say **"scene."** They complete their monologue and then in a very different physicality shrug their shoulders upward in apology and say **"scene."** This is not a monologue ending; it is an apology. It is as if the actor says to the teacher and class, **"I'm so sorry for making you sit through this awful monologue."** All of these artificial methods don't allow the monologue to end naturally. What then, should you do?

If we operate on the assumption that you are not directly addressing your classmates or teacher during your monologue, then ending your monologue is very simple. You complete the last line or action of the monologue and then allow a moment after to occur. This allows both the audience and whomever your character is speaking to to react to that last moment. You take this short beat, then change your physicality from your character's **back** to your own or neutral position and look directly at and acknowledge the teacher and class. This will tell them that the reality created for the character has now ended and that you are back within the reality of the acting class. You don't ask for applause or any reaction for that matter. All you are communicating to the class is that the monologue is now over. The teacher might say **"thank you"** and that is it. After your presentation, your acting teacher usually will comment on your performance, give specific notes or ask you additional questions. Remember, it is not a good idea to comment on your own performance because it is a losing proposition either way. If you say,

"Wow, that was terrible. I can't believe how bad that was." They may not have felt that way. Alternatively, if you say, ***"Wow, was that hot or what? I can't believe how well I just nailed it today."*** In this case, they may also not agree. Best bet is to not comment at all and let them do the talking. If you are asked to perform portions of your monologue again and are given notes, listen to them carefully and try to incorporate them into your second performance. Many times an acting teacher will give notes just to see how you take direction and incorporate their comments into your performance.

How to have fun at acting class

This last note will sound a bit cliché' but if you are having a good time your acting teacher and fellow classmates will be more likely to become engaged in the intellectual, emotional, physical and spiritual life of your character. In a recent acting class I taught, there was one student who prefaced all of her assignment as a "chore" that she really didn't want to do. This type of negativity sets you up to fail. In addition, if you feel good about what you are doing, you will do it better. Can you visualize that first moment you had the thought that you wanted to be an actor? Maybe you were watching television, a movie or a play. You sat in your seat and you thought to yourself.

"I can do that! I want to be up there on the screen or on the stage. I want to do it because it's something I enjoy. No it's something that I love. I love to act because it's inside of me and part of who I am. I can't think of doing anything else!"

Okay, so that seems a bit over the top. But didn't you ever feel this way at least a little bit. Well, I want you to go back to that personal moment for you. Go back to it and remember that you wanted to act because you love it and it makes you happy when you do it. Keep that always in your heart and find joy in what you do. Even if you don't get a part or you get your monologue assignment all wrong, it doesn't matter because there will always be another day, another assignment, another audition and another part to play. When you perform in class, have a great time. Be thankful that you have the opportunity to perform and share your talent with someone. This is not really advice, its common sense. But it goes to the core of why we act. We act because we love to act and that passion should be part of everything that we do.

THE MONOLOGUES

#1 SIGMUND FREUD AND REPRESSION

If I said: "Sigmund Freud?" You would say, "Yeah that's the psychiatry guy… the father of modern psychology who coined the phrase "repression." Freud believed that repression is an unconscious process in which we exclude unacceptable thoughts and feelings from our own consciousness and memory. We literally block memories that we do not want to remember. Let's see… what's a memory I don't want to remember? How about that Bugs Bunny raincoat with the floppy ears my mother forced me to wear on the first day of school in second grade? I really don't want to remember that.

(Beat)

Boy, Freud hit the repression nail right on the head with a sledgehammer… and he never even met my mother.

#2 SOMEONE

My life has been a composite of moments. Some were important but most have been nothing more than a reference point along my journey. I wonder if anyone thinks about their own moments that I had with them and now remembers **me** as someone special in their lives? Maybe they remember me as a person who was there and promised to fill an empty place in their lives but for some reason it didn't happen. I might have been someone they fell in love with but that I didn't even notice. I wonder where they are now and what they look like?

(beat)

Maybe they no longer exist… just someone, lost in time… vanished like a candle spent without ceremony. For me they remain a distant memory beneath a starless sky and someone I might have known.

#3 ANIMAL REPULSION

Okay, I admit it… I prefer the company of animals over people. I love all kinds of animals. Even the kind most people are repulsed by - like rats. Have you ever looked at one close, they are kind of cute. Ever see a rat's nose wiggle around when they are trying to smell something? You have to love that! And the possum? I mean, what is a possum anyway? I don't even think the possum knows if it's a rat, a cat or a dog. It just hobbles around like it has a stubbed toe. I think possums get a bad rap because everyone that sees one thinks it's a large rat. And if you can picture the size of a possum (about the size of a twelve-inch television) and try to imagine that it is a rat, that is one very large rat. Anything hobbling around that big can't be good. So we hate rats and possums. But I say we have to reach out to these misunderstood creatures. Make them feel not so repulsive. Just say hello and let them go on their way. Just like, you would do to a stranger on a train.

#4 WEARING GLASSES

What is it about glasses that make the people wearing them look like they are smarter? Does the logic go "if you wear glasses, you must read more books and therefore you are smarter and if the glasses are very thick, it implies that the person wearing them is a genius.

(Puts on glasses)

Now there's another way to think about this. "You wear glasses and then actually "feel" smarter. Let's see, I just put these glasses on and suddenly I feel clever. Go ahead, ask me anything you want except directions to somewhere. Guys don't ever ask for directions. It's not masculine to ask someone how to get somewhere. Guys have an intuitive sense of direction at all times. It's part of our "hunting" heritage. I am one of those people who always knows **exactly** where they are going. So, fire away… ask me anything you like.

(Beat)

I'm waiting. Nothing? I would like to stay and talk but should be on my way to the library to read some very thick books. Now, if I can only remember how to get there?

#5 LUCKY

"Lucky" is a great nickname for a dog. Especially a stray dog that is rescued from the pound. People would say, **"Wow, look at that stray dog now, boy he's really lucky."** Then, I met this guy at a party whose name was Lucky. At first, I figured he was just kidding me and that Lucky wasn't his real name. But everyone at the party called him "Lucky." So, I figured it was true. Lucky was a nice guy who said he was going to law school. Law school is really hard to get into, so Lucky was either truly **"lucky" or "very smart."** Then, I thought how would the world look upon an attorney named Lucky? What if being called "Lucky" by everyone might actually give him bad luck? What if every legal case he took he lost? How would that work? There would always be the never-ending pressure to come out on the top or people would say, **"Lost our case Lucky? Not "lucky" today? Better luck next time."** I still think Lucky is a stray dog's name. Also, I also think of "Lucky" in Pokémon. When this guy Lucky becomes a lawyer, that could be a problem as well. Wonder if anyone else will think of that?

#6 THE TAT

I just got this TAT on my arm. There is this guy in my Sociology class that is one of those real "musician" types with a nose ring and all. Maybe in a band? No, most definitely a singer in a band like Machine Gun Kelly. Last class, he kept looking over at me and I felt this pressure that I had to be musically cool for him to be into me. So, I bought a pair of jeans with holes in the knees and a very cool Rap Legends T shirt. When he came into class, twenty minutes late as always, he sat only two seats away from me and smiled when the teacher called my name. We really connected at that moment like we never had before, Then, I don't know, he started drifting away and started checking out this blonde sorority babe that was in the first row. I mean what's that all about? I just didn't see the connection there at all! So, I figured I had to go for broke and that's why I got this TAT on my arm. Just a small black rose. I just know it will get his attention when I see him in class again. I mean he's gotta see it right?

#7 IRON CITY – 1957 COUNTRY SQUIRE

When I was a kid, I used to ride in the back of my dad's 1957 Ford Country Squire station wagon. Its exterior was white with wood panels along the doors and the interior was pleated red and white seats. Every once in a while, my dad would fold down the rear seat which made the car feel more like a bowling alley than a car. When the back seat was folded down, the car seemed larger than life and full of possibilities. I would imagine it as an intergalactic space ship, a B17 bomber or with the help of a small plaid blanket a submarine. My all-time favorite thing to do was to lie on my back while my dad drove and look up through the rear windows. I watched the world go by upside down. The upside-down world of trees, clouds, power lines were all connected at abstract angles. The ground had a way of defining everything the same way; but when I viewed the world upside-down through the rear window of our Country Squire, trees danced lightly under a blue sky outlined by the never-ending sway of black power lines. As the AM radio played the Bobbettes **"One Two Three, Look at Mr. Lee**," I pulled the plaid blanket over my head and slowly went to periscope depth.

#8 KONG ISLAND – 1931

We moved up real slow as drums beat and a hundred primitives danced like monkeys around a burning fire. Joey started cranking the camera and got lots of swell footage of this chief wearing a monkey mask pounding on his chest. Then, the drums stopped cold and the whole lot of them looked at us like we're meat on a stick. When the chief hit me with a spear, we did the 23 skidoo right back to the boat and barely got out alive. Look right here at this scar from a spear they threw at me. Now everything's just swell! We're going to go back tonight. I just can't wait to see what's on the other side of the big wall they got running across the island and see what all that monkey dancing is all about.

#9 BABYSITTING

My parents have been up my butt about getting a part time job after school. So, I went to the mall last Tuesday and walked around but didn't see anywhere I wanted to work. I mean, how can you work at the mall? The mall is a happy place to hang out not for working. Then I went to Starbucks and Mickey "D"s but they said I didn't have enough experience. Really? How much experience do you need to pour a cup of coffee or put a burger in a paper bag? Besides, the kid that interviewed me at Starbucks asked for my number! Gross! So, I decided on a babysitting job watching little Edward here. I can't call him Eddie. His parents are really fussy about that and make me address him as Edward. But it's not so bad, except occasionally little Edward gets a bit fussy... like now! And the only way to get him quiet is to speak in a really high voice. (High voice) **Here you go, Edward. Peach your favorite. Here it come like a giant dinosaur flying in the sky! WAHCK! WAHCK! WAHCK! Open up! YEOW!** Maybe I should rethink this whole "babysitting" thing and check out the mall again. I was thinking Forever 21?

#10 SNAPSHOTS

I know most people today don't print snapshots They just store them in phones and the cloud. But not that long ago, people took snapshots and got them printed. The other day, I looked at some faded prints crammed in an old striped suitcase that was in the attic. They were stacked in neat piles representing both significant and nonsensical moments of my life. Lots of silly poses and smiling faces. Why are we always asked to smile when we get our picture taken? There are also the group shots, where I'm next someone I don't know or have forgotten. And every now and then, there is a snapshot of someone I **do** remember… quite well, who is no longer living. I look at those photographs a little longer than the rest and I try to put that person back together again and recall the moment I last saw them. Sometimes, no matter how hard I try, I can't recreate them. They have escaped my memory and the faded image I hold in my hand is all that is left. Why did people take snapshots anyway**?** They snapped them, look at them once, then packed them away in attics as forgotten moments. I was about to close the suitcase and put it away but instead dug deeper into the stack of snapshots. I was seeking proof of my living; that I existed, touched the lives of others and more importantly that I was loved. I guess… after **I'm gone**, someone will open this suitcase again and look at these old snapshots and see me… and like pieces of a mosaic, they will try to put me back together again… and remember.

#11 INVISIBLE

I was waiting on the fifteen items only checkout line at the grocery store, when I took just one small step to the right, like this (move to the right), to get a pack of breath mints. Then, stepped back again and BOOM, The woman that was behind me was now in front of me putting her Slim Quick Yogurt and Diet six pack on the checkout counter. I was just about to say something when she (without looking up at me) snapped: **"Sir, while you're there, can you get me a package of breath mints?"** Without thinking, I replied, **"Spearmint or Lemon?"** Counting her yogurts with her index finger, she replied, **"No, winter mint? Now you've made me lose count."** I apologized: **"I'm so sorry, doesn't seem that they have…"** She let out a breath: **"Forget it…"** She turned away from me as she swiped her credit card. That's when I decided to let her have it. **"Madam, you just cut in front of me in line. That was insensitive and rude."** She stopped what she was doing and turned back toward me and gave me a piercing look: **"Are you absolutely positive that there are no winter mints on that rack?"** Before I could answer, she shook her head and turned away, picked up her plastic bag and left. At that moment, I knew I had reached the true apex of evolution… I had become invisible.

#12 TEST DAY

I have a test today. Chapter 7 – The Ecological Health of the Planet. Who gives a crap about the Ecological Health of the Planet? Where all going to die anyway, so why should we worry about whether or not the planet is healthy. I mean the planet has been around for billions of years, who am I to mess with that? Okay, you're thinking, "If the class sucks, why don't you just drop it?" Right… but not so right. I have to take this class to graduate because my parents want me to get an A.A degree and then get a job. I already have a job working at the food court in the mall. I'm talking a career in culinary arts. So why do I have to do this school thing? So here I am, sitting here taking this stupid test. An essay? Prof never said anything about an essay. I am totally blank. I'll just raise my hand and ask to go to the bathroom. Should think of something to put down here by the time I get back.

(She/he raises their hand and mouths "I have to go to the bathroom.)

(Gestures #2 and exits.)

#13 THE FULL COLLEGE EXPERIENCE

I am at the start of my undergraduate education! Is that cool or what? I never thought I would have made it this far. There were some shaky moments back there in my high school Geometry and Chemistry Lab. But that's all behind me now. I'm at a four-year college and my parents are forking out some major bucks to send me to this Ivy League university so I can mature normally into adulthood, make life long career connections and lastly get a well-rounded liberal arts education. What's my major? That's easy… undecided. In fact, I don't have a clue about what I want to do with my life. So, instead of being stressed about all these "future" decisions, I'm going to take this extraordinary opportunity of attending college and never missing one toga party or sorority invite, become president" of a fraternity with "Chi" or "Kappa" in its name and most importantly acquire the technical skills to be able to pass a sobriety test after three hours of Beer Pong. This next one is a **maybe** but I hope to be able to name all the states in the union backwards while standing on my head and sipping a keg of beer through a small plastic tube and yes, I almost forgot, to strive for world peace! Now, that is what I call a full college experience.

#14 THE CLASSICS

I'm a college professor and the other day a student walked into my class wearing a Tee shirt with the words "French Connection" on it which made me think about the movie **"The French Connection"** with Gene Hackman chasing a wily drug dealer through the streets of New York City. Just at that moment, another student entered took her seat wearing a yellow ribbon in her hair. I couldn't help but think of the John Wayne western **"She Wore a Yellow Ribbon"** which was a larger than life cinema epic directed by John Ford filmed in Technicolor and part of a trilogy of films Ford made about the U.S. Cavalry. As I took attendance there was a student on the roster named Vivian Li made me think of Vivian Leigh as Scarlett O'Hara in **"Gone with the Wind."** I was making my way through the rest of the list of names but couldn't get the film out of my mind and climatic scene just before the intermission when Scarlet Ohara down on her knees in the barren dust of what was the grandeur of Tara eats a bitter root then says, (Southern dialect) "**As God is my witness, they're not going to lick me. I'm going to live through this and when it's all over, I'll never be hungry again.**" Wow, they just don't make them like that anymore. I opened my notebook to begin my lecture on Ancient Greece when I glanced up at the classroom clock… it was noon. **"High Noon."** (sings High Noon theme) Da da da dah… dee dah dah dah dah…. Now **that** was a classic.

#15 BRIDGES

I built a bridge to you every time you pulled away from me. Whenever you became cold and distant and I reached out to you and pulled you back. That's the way it has been for a long time.

But now, I am tired of doing all the work. Your distance is wearing me down and I'm starting to get the feeling maybe that you and I staying together may not be worth it. Just so you know, the next time you go distant on me, I'm going to let you go. I am not going to fill in the silence any more with smiles and warm touches, which are not returned. It will be just an empty space between us. There'll be no bridge to connect us from where we have been to what we may become. There will be nothing to hold us together to stop us from being apart.

#16 THE MESSAGE

Hello, I am away from the phone right now saving the planet and rescuing fur-baring creatures like dogs and cats from harm. It's not that I don't like reptiles or birds, but fur-baring animals are the most oppressed by their human masters. If this is George, please leave the keys under the mat and remember it's not your fault. It's really me. I find it almost impossible to commit longer than thirty days. Also, I don't want you to think I have anything against employees of the U.S. Postal Service or don't want you to deliver my mail any longer. I have a phobia of uniforms, which is rooted, to my childhood parochial school experience. And George, this doesn't mean we can't still be friends and go to the Woody Allen film festival together as long as you don't mind skipping **Annie Hall**. I absolutely will not sit through the kitchen lobster scene.

As, for the rest of you, that are **"not George,"** please speak slowly, leave your name and number and I will reach out to you as soon as humanly possible. Oh, almost forgot, if this is Dr. Woo at Izzy Zen Acupuncture Aroma Therapy Spa, I can't do next Tuesday because I will be on a vegan retreat upstate. When you hear the beep, you know what to do – Bye!

(Press stop record button)

(Exit)

#17 THE 13TH FLOOR

I stepped into one of those fancy office building elevators. As the doors closed, I was all alone checking myself out in the mirror and singing along with the overhead music "**Sometimes when we touch… the honesty's too much and I have to close my eyes and hide."** I noticed that the elevator was perfectly still and realized I forgot to press the button for my floor. I reached over to press my floor and realized there was no little shiny button for the thirteenth floor. They were all there "L" for lobby up to the nineteenth floor. The twelfth floor was followed directly by the fourteenth. No thirteen? That had to be for superstitious reasons. The unlucky number thirteen, Friday the 13th, Thirteen Apostles at the Last Supper, Apollo 13 and all that triskaidekaphobia nonsense. No matter what they did to avoid it, there was a thirteenth floor. The only difference was they didn't call it that. They called it the fourteenth floor. Then two questions hit me. **One:** what about those poor unlucky bastards that had offices on the on the fourteenth floor? Did they realize that they were actually on an improperly labeled thirteenth floor and (as luck would have it) could perish at any moment? And two, what floor was *I* supposed to get off at? Just at that moment, a bell rang and the elevator doors slid open – as I stepped off the elevator, I couldn't help but wonder if where I was standing was… ya'know… 13?

(Exit cautiously)

#18 SOLITARY

I am sitting by the lake on a summer afternoon thinking of you and see your face reflected in the still water sketched like a dream. But when I reach out, you are not there. I want to tell you that I'm sorry and wish I could have said that to you sooner. But that feeling is hard for me to acknowledge and I painted myself in a corner. Once I was there, I didn't know how to get out. I don't know what to do… now there is just silence. The sun is setting low making the hills draw a shadow on the water's edge as I sit in this gray stillness without you.

#19 PARTY ANIMAL

Party on! Not really… I can't talk very long because I have to get ready to go to this incredibly boring party and frankly, I'm quite pissed about it. You probably are thinking that I should just throw something on and go. But I am just in a "veggie" type of mood tonight. Just want to sit back in front of the TV and maybe watch an old movie, get a pizza. What's wrong with that? But, **NOOOOO** I'm going to this party because **I HAVE** to go - it's somebody's birthday… someone I don't even know… something like my girlfriend's boss's sister's best friend's roommate. Who gives a crap? Just look at me, I am all dressed up with my hair all lacquered down. I don't see why I have to do this… but if I don't go, there will be hell to pay. My girlfriend Louise will say… "Okay, fine… just fine… stay home and make me go to this party alone just like a dog!"

(Beat)

Alone Louise? Just like a dog. Really, what's so bad about that?

#20 STRIPES

I just love wearing stripes! Let me be more specific… up and down stripes. I don't like wearing thick sideway stripes because they make you look like a convict on a chain gang. However, I do love the visual affect created by a tasteful array of thin stripes – running vertically. Sideways stripes are just wrong. They make you look all horizontal, squeezed down by gravity and compressed into an out of focus blob! But stripes "up" and "down" make you ascend to a higher place… make you look longer… and let's face it… we all need to look a little longer. Walking around the streets striped tall, thin and above it all like a classical Greek statue waiting to be discovered.

(Pose, walks, turns then exits like a fashion model on a ramp.)

21 ELEANOR RIGBY

"Eleanor Rigby picks up the rice in the church where a wedding has been..." That Beatle lyric has always bothered me. Have you ever tried to pick up rice? Especially when it's mixed with all sorts of other organic debris like pebbles, sand, bird droppings or dirt. Rice mixed with grainy dirt; what good is that? What could you do with this kind of rice? Maybe, wash it then cook it? Plant it? No you would be able to plant it. I don't think so. I mean, picking up rice at a church where a wedding has been is at best a fruitless task, with no possible benefit to anyone but perhaps a symbolic one made by some lonely desperate soul who pathetically reaches out by performing this senseless ritual to feed upon some inert desire to touch even the smallest spec of humanity and thereby discover some meaning in their otherwise empty and hum drum life.

(Beat, thinking about this)

I think I just had an epiphany. I wish I had a pen or something to write this all down.

(Exits)

#22 MY LOCH NESS

You moved silently through
cold dark water like a dream
spun by Hypnos spirit.
Then for a moment under the starlit sky
you revealed yourself with an Aphrodite smile,
as hair like silk newly spun;
fell lightly upon your Madonna neck.
My mind's admonitions softened
in favor of my heart's desire.
As if my affection's gaze were madness
prompted by a fiery ambition,
I turned toward you to speak.
but found only blackness reveling upon itself
some darker fantasy spun fleetingly;
like a whisper too quiet to be heard.
Now I am left with an apparition's end
fallen upon a shadow everlasting,
I shall remain your plaintive seeker
forever
longing to see you again
my Loch Ness

#23 SHE PUT HER KNEE UP

We were at Starbucks just sitting and talking when she put her knee up to her chest and sat listening to what I said like I was a celebrity giving an interview. Meeting people is a total bitch. But occasionally you hit pay dirt. The only problem was I wanted to know more about her; but she wasn't a talker. She was a listener. I told her the story about when I was ten and how I got four stitches in my head when my older brother smashed a shopping cart into my head. She laughed at the end of the story and then pulled her other knee up to her chest and sipped her latte.

Then, nothing but complete silence. I decided to see how far it would go and we both sat there in in silence and smiled between sips of coffee. Still, there was nothing. Not a sound. Then without warning, she got up and left. Her seat was cool and empty, as if she had never been there. I sat back in my chair, put my knee up to my chest, and started to think about what had just happened. My mind wandered back to my childhood, when I was seven and I accidently swallowed a bee.

(Smiles)

Now that is a very cool story…

#24 A LINE IN THE SAND

Wow! I cannot believe this is happening again! Just when I start getting really into you – like wanting you to meet my friends and hang out; you go off and start making lots of rules that really piss me off. As soon as I let my guard down, let you in, you start screwing with me. Why can't you just accept me for what I am? I have been through this before and it is not going to happen to me again. I'm going to nip it in the bud and say what I really feel. I'm not going to worry about hurting your feelings or ruffling feathers. And if you don't like what I'm saying … then leave. This time, I am drawing a line in the sand.

#25 INDIFFERENCE

I called you several times last night starting around three thirty but you didn't pick up. I guess I could have left a message, but I figured **"Hey? You might call me back- all on your own."** But you didn't. Early this morning, maybe around five, I heard the sound of a car driving by my bedroom window and I jumped up to see if it was you but it wasn't.

(Beat)

Look I don't want you to think I'm high maintenance but I'm just looking for some contact here. I want something back. I am not just talking heavy conversations about love. Nothing as important as that. I'm talking about the small stuff. Like **"Hello, how are you?** Just a few words so that I know that I am in this relationship with another person. This is a relationship isn't it?

(Beat)

Right now, I will even take irrational anger or snippy sarcasm. But I can't go on like this. All I have is silence filling this empty space and your indifference.

#26 JUST THE FACTS

I just found my TV remote in the freezer. Ever wonder about those incongruous events that surround your day-to-day existence like finding your cell phone in your dog's water bowl, losing your wallet and then realizing it's been in your pants pocket the whole time or… finding the TV remote in the freezer. The real question is why do these things happen me? So, let me cut to the chase. Let's explore the facts. For example, the TV remote in the freezer… fact, I did open the freezer to get a chocolate Bon Bon at 2:00 AM and I might have had the remote in my right hand while I reached into the freezer with my left hand. But I needed both hands to open the Bon Bon box. So, it is possible that I placed the TV remote in the freezer to free up my right hand to grab a Bon Bon. Solved! Now about my cell phone in my dog's water bowl…

#27 ASCENDING

I broke up with my boyfriend the other day. I had an inkling that something was up because of the little things that I started to notice. When I asked him something, he would always reply in one syllable. I would say, **"You okay?** he would answer with an exhale **"Fine."** Also, when we walked together, he folded his arms like an Indian chief (like this) instead holding my hand. Then, about a week ago, there was a purple bra in his backpack. I wasn't spying on him or anything, I just needed a #2 pencil for my Crisis of the Planet class. Finally, we were walking across campus and I was talking to him about how I thought Coffee Bean and Tea was so much better than Starbucks. I stopped for a minute to tie my shoe and he just kept walking without me and never looked back. I didn't think about it much for a few days until I decided to check him out on Instagram. There was a picture of him smiling with the word **"Ascending."** Like I said, I had an inkling that something was up.

#28 STEPPING OUT

(Singing) Steppin out without my baby…. Steppin out with the bros." Yeah, that's it. Just dropped off my girlfriend Vicky at home. She's got a curfew – gotta be home by midnight. But not me. I'm a freshman at a community college! That's the beauty of having a girlfriend that still lives at home with her parents. She can't stay out late. Got to be home and keep Mom and Dad happy. It is definitely a benefit. I drop her off at her front door step -- all safe and sound on time and then I am off to hang out with the bros!

(Singing) "Hangin out with da Bros! with my baby safe at home…" Nothing heavy. Just hanging maybe chugging a few beers. Whatever? Only bad thing is, I can't stay out too late. If I'm late then my dad won't let me drive his car.

(Beat)

(Singing) Steppin out without my baby… yeah… not too late… cause will take away his car…

Whatever.

(Exit)

#29 WITTY DIALOGUE

Being married means having to attend boring social functions like a toddler birthday party or Grandma Bubba's funeral. You will do anything to get out of these functions like forcing yourself to vomit just before you have to leave, faking a bone fracture or staging your own UFO abduction. But these are risky choices. So instead, you **"tough it out"** drink a little alcohol and get through it. While you're there, it's always good to lean on something rather than sit. If you sit, it looks anti-social but if you lean, you can still be a body in motion while still conserving energy. What to lean on? A post, a chair, a table – if it's a funeral – don't lean on the casket. It may fall and you do not want to have to clean **that** up. If anyone approaches you and asks, "How are you?" Answer their question with a question, **"How am I? How could I be? But what about you?"** People usually want to talk about themselves anyway and this will allow you time to relax while they talk about themselves. Also, if you can, try to talk in a specific dialect. If you are asked, "How are you?" You might answer in a Scottish dialect: **"Hew am eey laddy? Hew culd I eyee bee? But reely whiie downt yuuuu tell mey a wee bit boot yuu?** This is what I refer to as witty dialogue. It will make the time go by faster or better yet, (if you are really lucky) you may never be asked back again. It's a win win situation.

30 DAY TO DAY MATTERS

I like to think of myself as an agent of innovation and social change that is a high-minded AND vested in the betterment of all humankind. I am kind to animals (except reptiles), respectful to the elderly even though they are always in a bad mood, loving and nurturing to children, patiently teaching them life's lessons and boy would I really like to teach some of those little ass holes some lessons. Especially those little crumb grabbing brats that can't keep quiet in restaurants or movie theatres. I am a responsible steward of the environment. I recycle all my paper products and try as best as time and money permit to be as "green.". I do as much as I can but the truth is there is no time because I'm too busy doing the day-to-day stuff to be diverted to helping some cranky senior citizen or some pain in the ass kid. And the environment? Do you really think recycling that coffee cup really matters or that anyone really gives a crap? Truth is no one cares and let's face it, **"Shit Happens"** on an ever flowing and continual basis and before you know it your bogged down with all the "**gotta do's"** instead of **"wanna do's."** I'd like to stay but I can't just stand around here talking to you all day. I've got stuff to do.

#31 HELLO

Really, I've never done internet dating… this is my first. I just find it utterly impossible to meet anyone… it's all so contrived. Please have a seat. There, doesn't that feel better? Good. Now about your "hello." First and foremost, I want to tell you that I am very uncomfortable with saying "Hello" right off. Really, we hardly know one another and I would not expect such familiar behavior from someone I just met. At first blush, I can easily say that I really like you at least what I know of you. You do look a bit older than your photo but I'm willing to overlook that detail. I can sense by your closed physicality and the way you are avoiding direct eye contact that you are not enthralled by our conversation. I'm looking for someone who knows where they're going in life… So, here we are. What shall be our next step?

Oh? You are getting up. Good start. Now, you are walking away… that is a positive physical action and is definitely a choice… Going… Going…. Going…Gone.

(Silence)

… and we were doing so well?

#32 SIXTIES ROCK AND ROLL DREAM

I had this wild dream last night that I was listening to Led Zeppelin's Black Dog. **"Hey, hey, mama, said the way you move, gonna make you sweat, gonna make you groove."** I'm singing along with the AM radio in a red 62 Corvette convertible top down, driving down a country road with the sun on my face wind in my hair. **"Oh, oh, child, way you shake that thing, gonna make you burn, gonna make you sting."** Sitting right next to me is this very hot blonde hippie chick in a tie die tee shirt, a headband and a red-feathered boa around her neck. I put the pedal to the metal and fluffy red feathers started flying all around the car. She sang too **"Hey, baby, oh, baby, pretty baby, Tell me won't you do me now."** Then, she leaned over and kissed me. At that moment, I woke up and I was laying in my bed looking up at the ceiling with my clock radio playing Black Dog. Even worse, it was eight AM and I was late for work. I sprung out of bed, threw on a pair of jeans and a tee shirt. As I'm going out the door, I notice a something floating on small beam of sunlight coming into my bedroom through a crack in the curtains. It was a red Boa feather just floating gently to the ground.

(Beat)

"All I ask for when I pray, steady rollin' woman gonna come my way."

(Motions playing the guitar rift from the song and exits.)

#33 YOU NEVER LISTEN TO ONE WORD I SAY

You never listen to one word I say because you're so wrapped up in yourself that all I can ever get out of you is a one-syllable grunt… and if I'm lucky, a head nod. Don't tell me you are a visual person and that your ability to listen is impaired. That's a load of crap and you know it!

(Beat)

I said, "**That's a load of crap and you know it!**"

(Beat)

Of what? A load of crap… C… R…. A…. P!

You see, this is what I have been saying. You never listen to one word I say!

Not one!

I said… not one! You are one "**sorry**" piece of work.

(Beat)

No, I didn't just apologize…. **I am not sorry**. **You're** sorry!

…and I am… outta here!

#34 FATAL ATTRACTION

Let's face it, we disagree on almost everything. What I like, you find boring and what **you** like, I find revolting to my core. It's not as if we were attracted to each other at one time then drifted apart. The truth is I have **always** hated your guts from the moment I first set eyes upon you. I detest the very molecules of air you breathe and exhale. If you died at this exact moment, I would laugh so hard that I would cry. If I got stuck sitting on top of a Ferris wheel for ten hours in the hot sun and I had to choose someone to be sitting next to me and I had to choose between YOU or a putrefied dead smelly corpse with worms coming out of its eyes and ears, I would pick the corpse! I hate the space you are standing in right now and anything you touch. Are you getting the picture? No? How about this? I would rather be force fed grainy feces that has been floating in a sewer pipe of a public toilet than smell your rancid body standing next to mine. Okay? Get the picture? Good.

(Beat)

I'm starving; you want to get something to eat and then a movie?

Cool. My treat.

(Exit)

#35 PASTORAL

James and I decided to commit and we have rented this house in the valley. It's nothing grand. Just a small one-bedroom house with a patch of weeds for a back yard. Now I don't want to make the backyard sound worse than it is. There are many possibilities for an individual with the right flair for design. It's surrounded on all sides by a tall over grown cherry wood hedge. I cannot make up my mind whether to do a veggie garden with a wooden bench nestled in a bed of rust colored river rock or go in a totally different direction. Get a dog! Nothing outlandish, just a medium sized nine-teen or twenty-one-inch shorthaired canine. Maybe white or a light tan… which would complement the green veggie garden and seating area. And maybe, to one side a self-circulating blue glazed pottery fountain. In addition, a birdbath would be a nice touch; either made of stone or bamboo with overhanging seed feeder or berry bush. To frame it all, some yellow and red annuals just to give it all a finished look.

#36 DECAY

I remember the very first time I saw you at the library. You were tapping a yellow number two Ticonderoga pencil with no eraser to the tune of Jingle Bells while you were studying for your History midterm. The tapping sound drove me crazy. I thought to myself, **what an annoying ass hole**. I must have said it out loud because you stopped the tapping and said **"Sorry."**

"Sorry" that's the first thing you ever said to me. Little did I know that it was all you would ever be. We saw each other almost every day the next two months and it was good. Not great, just good. Then, it all slowly started to fall apart. You started to change. Not showing up most of the time and when you **were with me,** your mind was always somewhere else. It was about that time that the lies started, and there were many, and each time you told me one you slipped away from me a little bit more. And when we argued, every **"sorry"** you professed became more meaningless until it meant nothing it all.

(BEAT)

And now… at this very moment, there is nothing left. Not even a memory of what we were. It has all vanished into a void like it never happened at all. Sorry.

#37 JULIET'S UNDELIVERED NOTE TO ROMEO

Entombed, I lay waiting and try to speak,
But I'm stilled in black's revelry cold
joyless repose; In finality I seek
the light of a warmer place and you to hold.
In silent prayer, I do commend this right.
Supplication calls upon what my lips cannot.
A blackbird's song and the morning light;
quickly to amend before it is forgot
I mistook this a dream wanting an end.
To be quilled by the quiller forthright.
Who scribes each stolen moment to defend
this silence two and forty till our flight
I fear not this sleep as much as our vow;
which time like a suitor may disallow

38 DRUNKEN SUPERMAN

(South Carolina dialect under a soft piano)

Bartender, I'm feeling a bit home sick. Can you make a Drunken Superman? You can? My lord, I am going to fall off this chair! I just can't believe you know such a southern cocktail. You do me no harm sir...

(Beat)

Everything in this city moves so quickly. My word... ten after nine. Where does the time go? It's so hard to meet people these days. The world is just not set up for human interaction. I'm from the south and back home in North Augusta, South Carolina; we still like to look someone in the eye when we talk to them. My name is Emily... and you are Richard? Please to meet you Richard. You are truly a gentleman.

(Superman cocktail arrives)

I declare this glass looks so pretty I feel like I should take a picture of it before I touch it! But you know what they say. **"No use sitting around watching the grass grow, Richard!"** You are so well mannered for a Yankee. Well, here's to you my only gentleman friend in this great big bustling city. Cheers!

(Drinks, slow fade to black)

39 THE SOLILOQUY

(Holding skull or other profound object)

To be… (Beat) Line…

(Whisper) "or…"

Or…Not… Line…

(Impatient whisper) "to…"

To be… or not… Line.

(Irritated Whisper) "To be or not to be… **that** is the question."

I didn't ask for **"that is the question."** It makes me look like I don't know my next line. I really **do** know it! I just can't seem to think of it right now. I mean, I **knew all my lines** when I was driving in my car on the way here. Am I going to get a low grade on this? I really need an "A" in this class… and it's really not fair if I get a low grade! I know my lines and I'll prove it to you.

(Beat, closing eyes and relaxing shoulders then exhale)

Okay, here goes…

(British dialect)

To be…! or not to be…. really a question I shan't answer? To bolder and buffer the slings and arrows of outrageous misfortunes as fire burneth….and caldron bubbleth. A rose by any other name is a still rose. But hence I say fi…? I say fo…? I say… **Nay**… we are all but gay players who strut and fret their stuff upon the stage in joyous proclamation **"June busteth out all over…. all over the meadow and the hill!"**

(Beat)

Scene! I told you I knew it!

#40 PEE SOUP

(Holding a cigarette)

I quit cigs last week, so I'm just holding this while I take my break. My feet are killing me. Don't know what it is about Fridays but they seem to creep up on you all at once and then it hits you like a ton a bricks. Friday is my hump day… once I get through Friday, I can get off my feet and relax. Only two more hours left in my shift… most of the time it goes fast, but tonight I think the clock is moving backwards. That old geezer sitting on table four is a real pain in the ass. He keeps sending everything back. Last time he was here, he stiffed me on the tip. He's gonna do it to me again tonight, I can just feel it. When he sat down, he gave me crap about the soup… said the menu board up there says **Pee Soup**. *"P E E…"* Woops! I musta been thinking of something else when I wrote on the chalk board. Now I gotta climb up there and fix it or he won't stop complaining. Maybe tonight, if he orders the "**pee**" soup, I'll give him the real thing.

#41 FIVE SMALL BITES

Here's a fitness tip for you. A great way to lose weight is to just take five small bites of whatever you're eating and then put the fork down then wait two minutes before picking up the fork again. When you pick it up again, you do five more bites. You can mix or match whatever you eat but all you can do is five bites then two minutes with the fork down. How do you know when two minutes goes by? Easy, sing Twinkle Twinkly Little Star to yourself twice and you should be good to go. So, what's the science here? I read somewhere, that by slowing down your intake, you get full faster. It literally, gives your stomach a chance to send a message to your brain that says, **"I've had enough don't send anything else down here"** Sheila at my Cardio Crash class does it and she is as thin as a string bean. She also may be anorexic but let's not get caught up in all the details. Just do five small bites… I promise you it will work… and that's all that matters. Right?

#42 WOLF

Monahan's Pub was a local watering hole that had a sawdust floor and a crowd of regulars who would line up against the polished mahogany bar backlit by a line of amber whiskey bottles. All of this gave the place a kind of homey feeling where a wayward soul could pour their heart out over a glass of Tullamore Dew or Redbreast 12. There was this guy who used to perch himself in the back at the end of the bar. He had shoulder length hair, a thick handle bar moustache, plaid shirt, worn out jeans and on his face, a pair of horn-rimmed glasses. He just leaned on the bar with both hands outstretched like he was going to do a push up. On the bar, in front of him was a glass of whisky. He'd stare at it then slug it down in one gulp and slam the empty glass on the bar. After that, he'd throw his head upward and howl like a wolf. When he finished, the bartender would pour him another whiskey and he would assume his original position; arms pushed back against the bar looking like a wolf in the desert silhouetted against a setting sun. His name was Ed but everyone at Monahan's called him **Wolf.**

#43 ROPE

I found this piece of rope outside on the floor. Someone probably cut it off a much longer rope and tossed this piece away. Can you guess how long this piece of rope is? Maybe about a foot and half long? But that's not the way it began. This piece of rope was part of a much larger piece. Maybe fifty feet long. Then, little by little over time, it was cut over and over again until this little piece was left and just thrown on the floor. Doesn't look like it can be used for much now. Too short and too old to do anyone much good. But I thought I'd bring it with me and give it a proper finish rather than just let it sit there on the ground.

(Hold rope reverently)

"Rope" Thank you. You've always were there to tie things down so they wouldn't blow away in the wind. You held everything in place when we couldn't and taught us all that we could work together. Now, all that's left of you is this small piece. Just a shadow of what you once were. But you are not forgotten and remind us all that we are part of something larger and are never alone.

(Beat)

Never.

#44 THE BACKSIDE OF YOUR HEAD

You ever look at the backside of your head? I mean I really never spent much time thinking about the backside of my head… I had all to do with trying to get the front side of my head together. I would look in the mirror before I went out the door and check myself out… teeth, hair, nose, ears, eyes and then be on my way. I thought I was okay but that was until I saw myself in one of those mirrors where you're able to see the back of your head at the same time as the front. Let me tell you, it was amazing. My head from the back looked flat matted down and as big as a basketball. My ears looked like a taxi cab going down the street with its doors open. I was in a state of shock thinking that all this time I was working on the front side of my head when I should've been working on the backside… that's the last thing people see when they look at you. And the **last** thing they see is what they remember the most.

(Beat)

Think about that, next time you look in the mirror.

#45 DOG'S FEET SMELL JUST LIKE POPCORN

Have you ever smelled the underside of a dog's foot? It smells just like popcorn. Just like the popcorn you buy at the movies. You know that fresh roasted smell smothered with butter.

(Beat – take a sniff)

I love that smell and that's probably why I like dog's so much because their feet smell like popcorn. I've never really been able to figure it out. They just do... it's just one of those scientific facts... dogs' feet smell like popcorn. It's a mystery... and breath... did you ever smell a dog's breath... is it heaven or what? Especially puppy breath... no matter what they eat... and believe me they eat lots of things they probably shouldn't... but their breath always smells... well... like puppy's breath. I think it would be great if people smelled like different foods. Imagine coming home after working all day and having your feet smell like pumpkin pie or vanilla ice cream? Wouldn't that be nice? Or maybe not... I guess that's not such a good idea after all.

#46 WHITE SILHOUETTE
WHITE SILHOUETTE (MALE)

(A lonely violin echoes in the distance)

Dance with me
up close
with our eyes touching
kindly
upon our souls
true intent
softly in the night

Dance with me
up close
underneath the stars and
moon
and blackened
night sky
your hand in mine

Dance with me
up close
spinning like lace
softly
through the sweet
night air
like an angel's wings

Dance with me
up close
my love only
one
spinning like a
an ephemeral
white silhouette

#47 DONUTS

(Enter carrying a donut)

You know what they say? You are what you eat. And eating one of these babies has got to be bad for you. You pop it in your mouth and swallow it down real fast because you don't want anyone to see you eat it because you feel guilty. You feel guilty because everyone says it's bad for your body and because they remind you about all the starving people in the world who eat less calories in a month then you're holding in your hand.

(Takes a bite)

So you eat it fast…. you gulp it down without really chewing fully and then it goes from your mouth down your gullet to your stomach where it's processed and shipped directly to your ass… and stored as fat. That's why, when they say you are what you eat. You know what I say about what they say? Get a life! You bunch of pencil thin, politically correct, schizophrenic, up tight carrot eating pain in the asses! Get a life! That's what I'd like to say. But you know what I do instead.

(Takes a bite.)

I gulp.

#48 TO DIE FOR...

Here we are... finally made it to the top! Welcome to **Celestial Hills Cemetery and Water Park** your gateway to eternity located in beautiful San Fernando Valley.

(Long gaze over a hillside)

Now this is a view "to die for." Just beyond that row of office buildings, you can see through the smog and clear across the valley. Now, the actual space we discussed is on the eastern slope overlooking the freeway. Not as desirable as this city view, but **still** a view. Make no bones about it, when it comes to cemetery plots, I have three words for you... Location... Location... Location. The market value on your investment can only escalate with the passage of time. If you purchase today, I'm able to throw in at no cost to you, the Tahitian Mist landscaping and a faux marble grave marker with embossed gold leaf lettering and when you arrive, you won't be alone. I don't want to be a name dropper, but your parcel is adjacent to several television celebrities. You can truly spend eternity among the stars! Right this way. Please watch your step. You can kill yourself trying to walk over these grave stones.

49 COFFEE PEOPLE

There are two kinds of people in the world Tea People and Coffee People. Tea people are left-wing tree huggers that think drinking decaf chai mint tea saves the planet. They get up on their tea box and preach that coffee people are responsible for oppressed masses living in third world countries who work long hours picking coffee beans for a penny per pound. Those are the Tea People. Coffee people are aware of the socioeconomic and political conditions on the planet but are not consumed them. They just love drinking coffee. Coffee is not just a drink. It's an experience that represents the passage of time perhaps with friends or loved ones, a physical state of being and more importantly a philosophy of life. Yes, it's true to be a coffee person is to know the ecstasy that can be found from that first morning whiff of a full bodied, earthy and dark and ferociously brewed cup of coffee. I am a coffee person and for myself, that first sip like a magic carpet, transports me on a mystical journey to the rustic rain drenched mountains of the Colombia where Juan Valdez (his head covered by a sombrero so as to not get too much sun) carefully hand picks each Columbian bean and places it gently in a hemp sack strapped to the back of his loyal donkey. I've seen his picture on a can of coffee. Valdez doesn't look exploited to me. In fact, he seems pretty damn happy and don't I deserve a little bit of happiness? So, I take another sip it's perfect. . . . and at that very moment in time, there is nothing else in the universe except me and my cup of coffee. The world is bright and full of possibilities and I'm ready to face the day.

#50 A. X.

Just got out of the hair salon with my stylist Zerlina. How do I look? First thing I'm going to do is go home and wash this stinking gel out of my hair and comb it the way I like it. Zerlina slicked it front to back and now I look more like Elvis than I want to. I made the fatal mistake by asking, "What's that you're putting in my hair smells nice?" A new product called A. X. as she placed a mirror in my hand so I could see the back of my head. I said something like... "fabulous!" Then, in one swift move, she snapped off the girly smock around me and asked, "How are you on hair products today?" Before I could answer, the woman at the register placed a pink jar of A. X into a small bag and swiped my card. Then BAM, I got the hairdresser hug "Bye love!" Before I knew it, I was out the door holding my bag of A. X. and thinking to myself, I really can't walk around the street looking like this. I have to get home and get this shit out of my hair and I mean now!

#51 GOODBYE

One thing that I just hate to do, is say goodbye. I don't like the good and the bye put together in just that way. There's such a finality to this combination. When you say good bye you're expressing first a parting and secondly an ending. That's where I have the problem. I don't like endings… endings of anything. I like to think of life as a continuous series of events and relationships that progress onward into infinity. They may ebb and flow but they don't end. So when I leave someone, I prefer to say, "I'll catch you later." As if to say until next time so we're not done. I like it better that way. Think about love ones, people that you have known that have died, have you ever thought about the last moment you saw them alive and what you said? What they said and how you parted? Ask yourself, did I say good bye? Did I say anything?

Think about that next time you leave someone. Catch you later.

#52 CONFESSIONS OF A SERVER

I can't believe it. The couple sitting at table seven is losing it big time. She just threw a glass of Cabernet in his face making his shirt look like a Rorschach test. At the rate they're going, they won't make dessert. I got the whole story when I brought their third round of drinks. She looked up at me and snapped, **"He told me he was going to divorce his wife - what a crock! That was five years ago!"** Then, she grabbed my arm. **"Do I look like an idiot to you? Well Do I?"** I said, "…of course not, would you like to hear about our specials tonight?" She just continued. **"Well, he thinks I'm an idiot!"** Then she let him have it with a twenty dollar a glass Cab. For a second, I thought he was going to toss his glass back at her. What can you say when something outrageous like that happens? I smiled politely and said, **"Let me check on your appetizers… I'll be right back."**

(Beat)

Shit…. This job is getting dangerous.

#53 THE BARBERSHOP

When I was a kid... my dad used to take me to a Barbershop. A modest three seat store front with one of those swirling red and white candy cane poles in front. No appointments... you just went in and had a seat. They had comic books to read while you were waiting and when it was my turn, they straddled me on a leather bench which sat up on top of the arms of the barber's chair. When I sat up there, I was as tall as the barber. He wore a white barber's smock which looked just like the one the pharmacist wore at the drug store... he cut my hair with scissors, made a slow line around my ears and then evened off the back with one of those electric clippers... used to tickle the back of your neck. To finish it off, he put talcum powder on my neck and some green slick on my hair. It would go on your hair soft but after a few seconds... it was hard as a rock. On the way out, you would get a piece of Bazooka bubble gum or a lollipop and you were out the door. That was it... done! The Barber shop.

#54 LAUNDRY

Let's face it… it's my own fault. When they called me and said they wanted me to work on campus today, I was so excited that I forgot to ask how much they were paying. I figured it was eighteen an hour and that's not bad when you figure all you have to do is sit here behind this table and smile at every everyone that passes by. I mean I'm an aspiring actor, I should be able to do that. It's just selling. But what am I selling? My job is to get (mostly guys) to sign up for a laundry service that picks up your dirty clothes and brings them back to you all clean in a bundle. That's it! Not very challenging for an aspiring actor like myself and I can make my own hours so I have time to audition. So, that's good right? But the real rip is they're only paying me ten bucks an hour! I wonder if they're going to take tax out of that.

#55 HOLD DOWN THE SEATS

When we go to the movies and sit down, why is it that I'm always the one that has to get up again, go to the concession counter and buy you a drink and popcorn because YOU have to hold down the seats. **Hold down the seats...** what does that actually mean? You're holding down the seats from whom? You make it sound like we are at war and you have to hold down the seats so these velvet-coated masterpieces don't fall into enemy hands. While I, the brave soldier, venture across enemy lines to get supplies. Just once, I'd like you to get the Diet coke and popcorn. I'll still pay for it, if that's what you're worried about.

Just once, I would like to HOLD DOWN THE SEATS.

#56 SITTING SOMEWHERE OUTSIDE

What a beautiful night sky. I just love to look at the stars and wonder about the universe… my life…. and… us. When I say us… I mean you and me… together. It's just a beautiful picture isn't it? However, one thing could make it better. The night air is a little chilly and I was wondering if I could borrow your sweater? I know what you're thinking that I should have dressed in layers so I would have my own sweater to wrap around my shoulders. But the truth is, I just didn't have anything to go with this outfit and now I'm cold! But you haven't offered your sweater to me and maybe you're thinking, this is the only way I'm going to learn to be more responsible and will know better next time. Something like that.

(Beat)

You don't look like you want to give that sweater up do you? So I'll tell you what, we can take your sweater and wrap it around both of us. Wouldn't that be nice?

(Beat)

Wouldn't it? **Well wouldn't it?**

(Folds her arms tightly and looks up at the night sky.)

#57 YOUR SPIRIT

Sometimes and only sometimes at night when it's quiet, I can sense your presence. I'm not afraid. It's just that one part of me feels warmer than the rest of my body and I imagine that it's you trying to touch me. When that happens, I can smell your hair just the way it used to smell just after you washed it when it was still wet and you would sit right next to me on the edge of the bed. Then, you're gone again. Yesterday you hid my house keys in the kitchen drawer because you didn't want me to leave. But, I didn't get mad because I knew you're just playing a joke on me. Sometimes, I hear your voice softly whisper my name in the dark.

(Beat)

…and just sometimes and only sometimes… in the shadows… from the corner of my eye… I can see you for a brief moment… You are just the way you were

(Beat)

and in that moment, we are together again.

#58 – THANK YOU

Well… thank you for a great evening. I think it's important for people to say **"thank you"** to one another. There is so little civility left in this world. I'm so sorry that I didn't wear a costume. When you said, **"dress up,"** I thought you meant… **dress "up!"** I had no idea you wanted me to wear a costume. I am so sorry about that misunderstanding on my part. I can't tell you how impressed I am with you're THE MIGHTY THOR costume. I especially love the blinking lights. Reminds me of Christmas. Oh, that's chest armor? There I go again. I just can't get anything right tonight. And while I'm apologizing, I wanted to tell you how truly sorry I am for dropping that plate of pasta on your lap. It just slipped out of my hands and was an accident. If the picture your friends took of you is posted on Instagram, I'm sorry for that as well.

(Beat)

Well… thank you again… no need to walk me to the door. I'm good.

Really. Just, thank you.

#59 MAN'S WORK

As a general rule I don't clean. I mean I take a shower every morning - well, most mornings - when I have time… and **if** it's not too cold outside… or if I don't get up too late.

If it's one of those **non-shower** days, I just do the under the arm thing and I'm out the door. But I digress.

I don't clean the place I live in. Never have. I use what I call the ebb and flow technique. I move stuff from one place to another to give it a different look. But cleaning… guys do not clean.

We're men.

We hunt.

We gather.

We ebb and we flow

Women clean.

(Beat… sniffs his shirt)

Bet I can still get one more wearing out of this baby

Then I'll throw it out… go into my closet and hunt me up another.

#60 WOMAN'S WORK

What is it with my boss? I can always tell when he doesn't shower. You can smell it as soon as he walks into the office. The sweet smell of cheap under arm deodorant hits you like a ton of bricks falling out of a ten-story window. You say to yourself **he probably got up late… and did the under the arms thing**. But you know the real truth is that he is just a lazy loser who didn't bother to take a shower. So you pretend not to notice and get through the day.

(Beat)

Women are cleaner than men. I know men have that whole **hunter gatherer** excuse. But let's face it, when was the last time a guy ever had to hunt and gather anything? They just leave it all to us. We have to clean the house and go to the store. We do the hunting and gathering. We bring the food home, have to cook it and then clean it up. Why? Because that's woman's work. And that's the way it is and that's the way it will always be. But men can you do us women just one favor? Can you try taking a shower once in a while?

#61 DILLY DALLY

I'm one of those people that likes to get things done. Every day, I make myself a list… and one by one, my favorite thing to do is to check things off of it. Did this. Check. Did that. Check! I love to say, **"check!"** The list gets shorter and I have a sense of accomplishment and mobility. I feel like I'm going from one point to another. **"Progressing."** So the one thing that makes me crazy are people who waste time. You know who you are. You love to **"dilly dally"** your day away wandering from one point to another like a pinball machine. You start lots of things but never finish any of them. I don't know why? You drop one thing before it's completed and go onto the next. You are a tangled ball of incompletion! All you do is dilly dally…The result, nothing gets done. I just had to get that off my chest. Okay? Check! There, I feel better already!

#62 STEPPING ON THE CRACKS

Have you ever heard of the silly superstition that stepping on cracks on a sidewalk might be drawing you into the gap between the earthly and the metaphysical realm? If you step within one of these spaces, no matter how narrow, it could bring misfortune to you or your family. Pretty crazy eh? Well, the other day, I was walking on the sidewalk just doing an errand when out of nowhere my right foot got caught on a crack in the sidewalk. I fell down and landed on my elbow. At first, I just thought it was a little slip, but then about an hour later I couldn't bend my arm. Well, you guess it, I broke my elbow and had to walk around with my arm sticking out like a Nazi salute. Made lots of interesting new friends. But, from now on, I pledge I'm going to take superstitions more seriously.

(looks around)

Now if I can only find something wooden to knock on.

#63 PEACE

It's finally quiet… I don't think I could have taken another second of all the noise, constant bickering and the slamming of doors when we argue. I hate the sound of a door slamming. It's so final. So closed to any possibility. It locks the energy into the room and prevents air from circulating. Now, it's quiet, the lights are lower and I can feel each breath enter my body and then go back out again. The quiet envelops me. I can almost hear my heart beat. There it is. And the tension in my chest is going away. The quiet slowly surrounds me with a stillness I've never felt before… then blackness. I'm finally at peace.

#64 THE VIETNAM WAR AND THE FORT HAMILTON LAMENT

When I was a young man back in the crazy nineteen sixties there was a war going on in Vietnam. Most young American men didn't care about what was happening over there. They were more interested in doing what young men liked to do… have fun. The government had different ideas about that and set up the draft. So, if you weren't rich or disabled you were going to be drafted and get an all-expense paid trip to Vietnam. I got my notice to report to Fort Hamilton in Brooklyn, New York. I remember showing up there and having to strip down to my underwear so they could check me out. It was a humiliating experience, and when it was all said and done, I found myself, still in my underwear, waiting on a long line. When it finally got to be my turn, a straight-faced sergeant stamped my papers and said **"1Y Rejected."** I was a little put back. I was in excellent physical condition and couldn't help but ask why. I said **"Why?"** He looked at me like I had a disease **"You have flat feet! We'll call you if they attack Jones Beach. Now get the hell outta here!"** I was pushed out the front door like I was a piece of unwanted trash. After it was all over, I sat on the curb looking down at my feet and wondering what I would do next.

#65 PALACE HOTEL- NEW YORK CITY

Check out this view! I'm on the 40th floor of the Palace Hotel looking out at the New York City skyline and below me I can see the roof of the Saint Patrick's Cathedral. When you look down at the cathedral from above you can see that it is shaped just like a Christian cross. I wonder if they did that on purpose? Then, there are people below down in the street that look like ants walking on a donut.

(Beat)

Makes you realize just how small we actually are. I mean small in comparison to our achievements. All these tall buildings… and cathedrals shaped like crosses… built by all those little people small as ants. Makes you stop and wonder.

#66 HOW DEEP TO DIG A HOLE

When I was a little kid, I used to bury my toys… pretty much like a dog buries a bone. I'm sure there's some sort of physiological explanation for it. I would bury my toys so I would always know where they were and that they were safe. I struggled with making the decision about how deep I would have to dig to insure that the toy I was burying would remain safe. I thought, the deeper the hole, the safer but I didn't want to dig so deep that I wouldn't be able to find it again. What good would that be?

When I think about it now, I'm still digging holes… not real holes but the emotional kind. I don't have many friends but when I care about someone, I want to keep them close and safe and don't want to share them with anyone else.

I moved away from my childhood home when I was ten, I often wonder if all the toys I buried in those holes I dug in the backyard are still there? And if someone found them, would they wonder how they got there. If I ever get back that way, I should go knock on the door and ask.

#67 LISTENING

Have you ever pretended that you're listening to someone speaking when you're not? They're talking, their lips are moving and you look back in earnest. Sometimes you even nod in agreement while they're rattling away - talking about something you don't care about. They might even be complaining about the fact that no one ever listens to one word they say. While **you** in your mind are \catching a wave on a surfboard in Hawaii.

(Beat)

And when they tap you on the arm and say, **"Are you listening to me?"** You reply, **"Absolutely!"** They smile back at you and continue and you… earnestly nod in agreement… as you catch another wave.

#68 BAD HAIR DAY

I don't know about you but I don't wash my hair every day. Do you? I'm not even sure I should be saying this to you. It's kind of personal. Well, do you? Wash your hair every day? Okay, I can appreciate your unwillingness to share. But looking at it… up close… your hair looks a little flat. It doesn't have that fluffy just washed look. I'm not sure if you really want it that way or not. Please don't take this as criticism.

So, did you? Did you wash your hair? You did! Okay then.

No, it looks fine. Not really flat at all. Now that I look at it, it's kind of fluffy in the back. Yeah right there where it's sticking up… right next to the bald spot.

(Beat)

Hey, no sweat… it's not really **that** bald. Maybe pushed over to the side a little too much. You might just be having a bad hair day.

#69 DOG PEOPLE AND CAT PEOPLE

Okay, I'll admit it. I'm a dog person. It doesn't mean that I don't like cats. Cats are cool but I relate to dogs better. Dog people tend to hang out together. They support one another in their "**doggedness**" and are more co-dependent on other dog people. You'll find them at coffee shops, restaurants and parks with their canine friends trying to connect with other dog people. Dog people need to be told they are okay and that's because of their dogs, the world is a happier place. Now, cat people… they don't care. They are mostly loners with no real friends who pretend to be popular when the truth is… nobody likes them. Dog people carry pictures of their dogs around with them in their smart phones. They talk to their dogs as if they were human "**See Jeffery wag his tail? That means he wants his cappuccino with no foam.**" Cat people rarely take their feline counterparts anywhere. That's because a cat really has very little use for a human contact. Cats use humans for a modicum of shelter and food. Other than that, a cat could care less. Dogs are **needy** companions who constantly require the verbal praise of their masters. Cat people just open the door and let them out not knowing **when** or **if** they will ever return.

Like I said, I'm one of those dog people constantly reaching out… and hoping… to connect… to someone… anyone… who is just like me.

#70 - LIVING INSIDE A HEFTY BAG

Ever have somebody sit near you and the next thing you know they're coughing up something… awful, then sniveling all over you?

Like this…

(Cough up something)

Then snivel

When they do it, they sort of reach over toward you and then let it go. Why don't these people stay home if they're sick? Nooooo! They have to be right next to you! Then, there's another cough and then a snivel and let's not forget the wipe. They wipe their nose with their bare hand and then dry it off by rubbing it on themselves or even worse a door handle or the arm of a chair. I'm telling you it's dangerous out there.

(Beat)

Next time I leave the house, I'm going to wrap myself in a Hefty bag…. And maybe then I'll stand a fighting chance.

71 VISUAL AUDITORY

A true **realist** experiences the world objectively through their five senses of sight, touch, taste, smell and hearing. But the truth is our senses are not all equal. Some people are **visual** and connect to everything they see. They won't remember your name but they **will** remember the color of the sweater you were wearing when they met you. Then, there are the auditory people who just hear it once and can recite it word for word! I hate those people. You really have to watch what you say to them. The toucher-smellers are a little weird because they have to **touch and smell** everything to connect to it. Don't go to a nice restaurant with one of those people. They pick up their food with their hands and sniff it before they eat it.

Which one am I? I'm an auditory person. I need to hear things to validate them. The other day, I told my (girlfriend/boyfriend), "**You never tell me you love me.**" (He/She) looked at me and said, **"Are you kidding? I washed your car yesterday! Didn't I?"** You see? That was a visual response. They wanted me to **see** what they did. But I wanted to **hear** something from them… not see it. I wanted to hear the word **love.** I'm a word person… and words are important to me. What they did was **show** me love. Who the hell needs that?

#72 WASH YOUR HANDS

No matter how old you are, some things just stick in your head and you never can forget them. When my mother would call me for dinner, her voice rang high over my head **"Wash your hands!"** She would say it deliberately with each word standing out on its own **"Wash... Your... Hands... "** She held out the word **hands** a little longer. Then, I would wash my hands. You might be thinking that this was something that she only told me as a child. No way... she kept saying it to me even when I became an adult. To say the least, it stuck. My mother passed away several years ago but I can still hear her voice calling out to me from beyond. **"Wash... Your... Hands.... "** and you guessed it. I still wash them. Thanks mom... for turning me into Howard Hughes... and the compulsion I feel the moment after I shake someone's hand to immediately scrub down like a surgeon. As I scrub, I still can hear your voice... **"Wash Your Hands!"** Sorry, I hope I didn't get too carried away. Did we just shake hands... you know just a moment ago... when we first met? Gotta go... I'll be right back.

#73 LITTLE WHITE LIES

Little white lies are what you say when you don't really want to say the truth.

Why can't you say the truth?

You can't say the truth because you feel you should only say nice things or say nothing at all. That's what Thumper the rabbit said in **Bambi.**

Or because

You don't want to deal with the blowback.

Or even worse

You don't have a clue what the truth really is….

So you don't know what to say…

Like not knowing the difference between the color orange and red

Or, even worse…

Being afraid to say anything.

#74 BLOCKED

O M G I can't believe you BLOCKED me. I've been following you for at least ten months… maybe a year. I know I haven't posted much. But I did **"like"** your post about the starving puppy you found in the Bloomingdale's bag. I thought it was sweet that you adopted it and I am really sorry you got kicked out of your apartment. I hope it wasn't the **"Puppy Balloons"** I left outside your apartment door? I mean I know a lot of people who have pets in places that say they don't allow pets still have them anyway and they're fine. The **"No Pet"** rule is usually not the type of thing that you would get kicked out for. I hardly know you other than that one time we spoke in the elevator when I dropped that bag tomato soup and stained your paints. That's really how all this got started. I looked you up. It was that simple. Remember? And now… without warning you blocked me!

O M G, I can't believe you would do that after all we've been through.

L O L

#75 - HAPPY FOR YOU

I'm so happy for you! Congratulations! It couldn't have happened to a better person. You worked hard and really had it coming to you.

(Beat)

Okay, I have to admit I'm a little jealous. Just a little. But nothing I can't handle.

(Beat)

Well okay, I'm a little miffed. I guess some people have all the luck and then there's the rest of us… who can't get a damn break if their life depended on it. That's me… I'm always at the **right place** at the **wrong time**… or even worse…. the **wrong place** at the **wrong time**. It really sucks to be me!

(Beat)

But… I'm so happy for you!

#76 CONTEMPLATION OF SELF

You ever feel that no matter **what** you do it's never enough? That you never quite achieve the intended goal that you set out for? It can be anything big or small. Going on a diet, working out at the gym, making money or it could be a very slight insignificant goal such as making a list of things to do and checking each one off as you do it. But what if you make a list of five things and only do four? As you do each one, you get an uncomfortable feeling within yourself that is so disturbing that you're not going to make it to the end of the list. Instead of celebrating what you have accomplished you focus on that one incomplete item. This unsettling feeling keeps growing every waking moment of your life in contemplation of your self-condition. You are literally consumed by an aura representing your own self-loathing. It's an endless downward spiral into the darkness with only momentary snippets of sunlight coming through the clouds. Then, the morning sun warms your face and for that brief moment, and you find comfort. But only for a moment… then it starts all over again.

#77 DREAMING OF PARIS

Going to work… the same as every other morning. The train rolls into Penn Station. I walk up the stairs from the platform toward the street level. As I go up the escalator the air is filled with the aromas of diesel smoke, grease, brewing coffee and donuts. I've made it to the street and head to my office. I stay there all day until it's time to leave. On my way home, I do the same thing… only in reverse. I ask myself what I did during the day but I have already forgotten. I sit, in my seat on the train and the same people I see every day wear the same grey clothes smelling of cheap cologne and mothballs. There's the guy that pretends to fall asleep on the shoulder of a woman sitting next to him. She tries to lean away, but there is no room. Just to the left of them I see a young woman wearing a sweatshirt, with **"Dream of Paris"** written on it. I smile at her and sigh, **"If I only could."** She smiles back at me as the clicking rhythm of the train on the track lulls me to a soft sleep. **"If I only could."**

#78 ROMANTIC

Okay, breaking up sucks! But I am really pissed right now. You know what she said to me? **"Jeffery, you're just not romantic!"**

Romantic? What's that supposed to mean anyway? So, I asked, **"Romantic?**

What can I do to be romantic?"

She looked at me then without a beat started to cry. Through her tears I could hear her say, **"Taking me on long walks on the beach… when it's raining, watching Twilight movies and holding me close when I'm scared… and lastly… eating warm pizza in candle light."**

(Beat)

Now I don't know about you, but the "pizza…"

That's romantic.

#79 DUMB WAYS TO DIE

Dumb ways to die.

Eating a rusty nail.

Jumping out of a plane… without a parachute.

Kissing a cobra… right on the lips… and slipping your tongue in its mouth.

Sticking a fork… repeatedly… in a plugged-in toaster.

Watching Twilight movies… and eating microwave popcorn… for 24 hours straight.

Walking… in Central Park… at three in the morning… singing "I'm in the money."

Brushing your teeth… with super glue.

Sitting in a crowded jail cell… humming… "I'm in the Mood for Love."

Wearing a Star Trek costume at a Star Wars convention.

Dating someone… anyone… that's a serial killer. Then trying to break up with them.

Sticking a #2 pencil up a polar bear's ass… and waiting.

Sneezing so hard while eating spaghetti… that the noodles come out your nose.

Hiding a tarantula in your underwear… while going through an airport pat down.

Using a chain saw… to give yourself an eyebrow trim… in the dark.

Going up to a bank teller… wearing a bag over your head… singing the Ludacris rap song… "Stick em Up bitch! Stick em up!"

(Music plays – Ludacris's Stick Em Up)

(Exit)

#80 IF I COULD ONLY BE THIN

You ever notice that thin people always get everything they want? Life seems to always go their way. Think about it. All the movie stars, rock musicians and what about all those fashion models? Thin! I guess the way the universe works is… the thinner you are the more you get. You ever see a chubby person get a break? No way… it's the back of the line for them. They are destined to live mediocre lives at best.

(Beat)

Now take me… I'm hardly overweight. But, let's face it I'm not thin. I'm in the **"normal"** slightly chunky category. And really, I don't eat that much. It's just everything I eat goes directly to my stomach and ass. Just look at me. What do you think? How do I look? You think I look fine? Why am I not surprised? That's what everyone says. But let me ask you this. Would you like me better if I were thin?

(Beat)

I knew it! How about **really** thin? Look I'll bite on my cheeks, pull in my stomach and stand on my toes. Now, what do you think? Do you like me more? Well, Hello? Where did you go? Shit.

(Bites cheeks, sucks in stomach, tip toes and exits.)

Printed in Great Britain
by Amazon